Don't Laugh Till He's Out of Sight

written and illustrated by
Henry Brewis

Farming Press

First published 1984
Reprinted 1985, 1986, 1987, 1989, 1991

British Library Cataloguing in Publication Data

Brewis, Henry
    Don't Laugh till he's out of sight.
    1. Agriculture, – Humour
    I. Title
    630'.2'017

ISBN 0-85236-153-X

Published by:
Farming Press, 4 Friars Courtyard, 30–32 Princes Street,
Ipswich IP1 1RJ, United Kingdom.

North American Distributor:
Diamond Farm Enterprises, Box 537, Alexandria Bay, NY13607

Typeset by Galleon Photosetting, Ipswich
Reproduced, printed and bound in Great Britain by
BPCC Hazell Books,
Aylesbury, Bucks

DON'T LAUGH TILL HE'S OUT OF SIGHT

By the same author:

Chewing the Cud
Clarts and Calamities
Funnywayt'mekalivin'
The Magic Peasant

Preface

The book is a compilation of my writings from earlier publications now out of print, together with some new material and other pieces which have appeared in farming magazines over the past few years (NFU *County Journals, Farmer's Bulletin,* etc.).

They are linked to form a 'tongue-in-cheek' guide to the would-be peasant, perhaps a source of reassurance to any established peasant feeling low, and hopefully amusing to anyone who sees farming as an interesting (if at times ridiculous) way to almost make a living.

H.B.

Introduction

If I was a rich man
with elegance and charm
you wouldn't find me plodgin'
round a cold and clarty farm –
farming is for poor men
who only curse and swear
and those who make a fortune
are exceptionally rare . . .

It's generally accepted that people achieve very little on an empty belly.

To build a house, paint a picture, sweep the streets, or even stand in a dole queue, – y' gotta eat first.

Trade Unions can argue their special cases, and hold society to ransom until all the politicians lose their voices, – but without the occasional sandwich none of us function very well.

It would seem reasonable therefore to argue that farming is the most important profession, and (if only by a short head), probably the oldest too.

Once upon a time of course almost everybody was a farmer, or at least a peasant of some sort, – but now after a few industrial revolutions, the odd war, index-linked pensions, massage parlours and multi-storey car parks, the peasant population has shrunk to no more than two per cent of the electorate.

And yet almost everybody is still a peasant at heart. Lock man up in darkest suburbia, semi-detached, centrally heated and superannuated, and he will look for an allotment. a

1

garden, somewhere to walk his whippet, take his family for a 'run' in the country, – and very often *wish* he'd been born the son of a peasant.

And therein lies one of the peculiarities of modern life: almost everyone who isn't a farmer longs to be one, – while those who *are*, insist, some of the time at least, they'd be far better off doing something else.

But town and country could never swop. The peasant would go to pieces in the High Street, and however wistfully the 'townie' may dream of life beyond Sebastopol Terrace, – he really knows nowt about it.

His (and her) technicolour vision of farming is often based on no more than a sunny Saturday afternoon picking brambles in a wood, eating a 'free-range' egg with a bright orange yolk, or watching doe-eyed cows crossing the road on a summer evening.

In the eyes of many it's a life still spent under a cloudless sky, idyllic, pure and simple, in the company of warm woolly animals, and enriched with a fortune in subsidies from a leaky Common Market kitty. Farmers hunt foxes, shoot pheasants, drive big Volvos with a labrador on the back seat, wear brown tweed suits with green wellies, – and grumble all the way to the bank.

This somewhat unrealistic and confused image has been largely created by a growing array of parrot-brained politicians, bobble-hatted bird-watchers, card-carrying conservationists, endangered television producers, hairy poets, – and an endless supply of children's picture books. Books that for generations have shown Larry the lamb, Rover the dog, and Percy the pig, all living with their little friends in a pastoral paradise watched over by a rustic old nit-wit with the IQ of a breeze-block, and a vocabulary limited to 'ooh ahr', and 'git away bye'.

Mind you it must be said that farmers themselves do little to correct or rationalise these images. Even those connected with the industry who have written something on the farming scene invariably miss the opportunity to 'tell it as it is', – warts, warble-flies and all.

We either get the romantic epic novel of bold young Sir Timothy rolling about in the hayshed with the fiery well-endowed milkmaid who turns out to be the result of a tempestuous affair between Lady Daphne and the rabbit-catcher, – or a boring great encyclopedia on 'Successful Silage Making for Beginners'.

It's perhaps not surprising then that envious observers are left with the impression that farming is practised by a mixture of ageing be-smocked simpletons with dog and stick and thirty-year-old whizz-kids with a thousand acres and two suits who have probably inherited the land (and the suits) from a long line of country gentlemen stretching back to the robber barons.

The truth is that although all sorts of contradictory examples can be found in the business, the real unexpurgated pageant of farming revolves around the broad beam of the traditional peasant, a working bloke, an umpteenth-generation survivor who'll never make a fortune. He's not really ambitious enough for that, or devious enough, or lucky enough, or whatever it takes. But if the sky ever falls down, it'll almost certainly miss him, – and bury the 'clever buggers'.

He's a grumbler right enough, but a 'stayer' as well. When things go wrong (and as this book will suggest, they do), he blames the government, the weather, God, French peasants, British Summer Time, sheep, the NFU, his dog and the wife, though not necessarily in that order, – and starts again.

Only on rare occasions will he allow himself a cautious optimistic smile. After a good price in a bad trade at the mart perhaps, or having harvested a field of barley the day before a 'shake-wind', watching a growing calf or a shrinking overdraft, or in the company of a neighbour who's just had a disaster, and is silly enough to come looking for sympathy.

He considers himself very fortunate to enjoy one of those a year!

And yet the myth persists, – any fool can be a farmer.

The following pages therefore will endeavour to enlighten

those daft enough to be contemplating a career in peasantry, pointing out in a totally unbiased fashion the hazards and traumas that will be faced along the way.

What is a Peasant?

It has been said that farming is not so much a job, more a way of life, – and you've got to be born to it. The right 'breeding', the right attitude are undoubtedly important.

At worst, somewhere in your veins, there should be at least a few red corpuscles from a peasant ancestor, – even if he was only some long-lost rural rake who chatted up your grannie before marching off to World War I.

Put it another way, – a Clydesdale never won the Derby, and not many ballet dancers end up as farmers (or vice versa).

However from a distance, or from a passing car on a fine day, farming can look deceptively easy. More than one eager entrepreneur, having cleverly contrived his fortune from the wicked city, has promptly lost it in a wet lambing field or a cold mart.

It's rumoured that real peasants are actually born wearing a cap and wellies, and carrying a stick.

Their mothers may hotly deny this of course, but the fact remains that the true fledgling farmer is readily recognisable at a very early age. It's not unusual to see an auld-fashioned four-year-old, working and sounding just like his father. Chances are he can count the hoggs on the turnip break before he gets to the classroom, – and swear fluently before he can read a word from *Janet and John*.

At school he's not really expected to shine, – an 'O' level in metalwork will class him as an academic. Anything more, and it's assumed he's too clever by half, and not suited to agriculture at all. Thoroughly disappointed, his grief-stricken parents may even be forced into the added expense of the Sixth Form, and possibly University, in order to get

5

their 'poncie' no-good waster into an 'inferior' townie job.

Ideally the quicker 'son and heir' leaves school and does 'something really useful' (like muckin' out a byre), the better and cheaper it is.

It also ensures that young Willie (or whoever), never has the time or the inclination to consider seriously any other less worthy form of employment.

From this you can assume that peasants consider themselves to be a race apart, the chosen few, – the rest of the population, 'gentiles', unable to discuss major issues of the day like Yellow Rust and Staggers, and consequently of little real value to the nation.

The odd exceptions will include the bank manager, who is reckoned to be on a par with the Pope, and similarly infallible. The accountant too is viewed in some awe and compared favourably with Einstein, because he apparently understands VAT and can do long-division sums. And of course the vet, but only when the patient lives.

The peasant may also show *some* grudging esteem towards another farmer, – provided the bloke is an immense age, and can value store cattle in a field on a dark night, to the nearest fiver.

Younger farmers can seldom expect unqualified respect from their elders. If they are somehow successful too early, it will be assumed they've cheated, i.e. inherited some money, – and if they are seen to be struggling the diagnosis will probably be, 'too much pop and not enough graft'.

The established peasant then is a hard man to impress. A newcomer to the industry, or even an immigrant peasant from another farming district twenty miles away, will have to work like a demented beaver, top the mart at *not too* regular intervals, somehow let it be known that his barley yields are in excess of three tons, make beautiful hay while all around make 'muck'; never ask for credit beyond the confines of the bank manager's office; clip a yow in three minutes (without removing her lugs); lend his wuffler to all his neighbours and borrow nothing in return; publicly tell the Hunt to get off his winter wheat, – and

6

'assassinate' at least one worm-drench rep in full view of the postman!

If he can do all this and a bit more, consistently for about thirty years, he *may* be accepted into the 'brotherhood', – but it can't be taken for granted.

However if he can but *survive* for this period, more or less sane and solvent, without incurring the wrath of the Lord, or the Northumbrian Water Authority, – there is a fair chance that the foundations will have been laid for a modestly successful career.

It must be pointed out though, primarily for the benefit of the woman in his life, – that long before this has been achieved there will be two fundamental psychological changes in the man.

Firstly, very early in his business life if there's to be any hope for him at all, he will develop a peculiar mental disorder, known in the trade as 'selective amnesia'.

This will become an integral part of his make-up, and is absolutely essential to farming at any level.

'Selective amnesia', as the name implies, permits the peasant to forget, or at least modify, many of the disasters that will surely befall him, – and, when necessary, allows him to embellish the occasional triumph.

In short it is a euphemism for telling lies, or at least half-truths, not only to others but to oneself as well.

For example, after the most disastrous lambing in years, during which half the yowes are geld and the other half abort, the tup is shot, and the collie dog runs away with a lurcher, – the peasant must be able to rid his mind of these sordid little details, take a deep breath and talk in terms of 'a canny lambin' regardless. If not, he can become suicidal or crackers within weeks.

Similarly when all around are claiming some astronomical winter barley yield, he must, no matter what the facts are, conjure up his own mythical figure to compare favourably with the mythical norm. An actual 2.6 tons per acre can easily be amended to roughly three', – or, if necessary, to 'well *over* three!'

All these 're-adjustments' must be done without the suspicion of a smile.

Secondly it is inevitable that the emerging peasant will become as mean and miserable as a constipated vulture in all matters concerning domestic expenditure.

There is very little the devoted wife can do about this except inherit a fortune of her own. She can rant and rave, or slink about in a see-through fertiliser bag, whispering warm sweet rubbish into his ear, – but to no avail.

She must simply accept that he will readily spend a five-figure sum on a technicolour combine, hundreds on a shampooed Charolais, or thousands more on a tractor, or whatever he deems necessary for his outside empire, – but ask him to replace the mat on the back door and his health will be seriously affected. He'll cough and wheeze and splutter, apparently on the brink of cardiac arrest and financial ruin, – and may not speak for a week or two.

So do you still want to be a peasant? Is it in your blood?

Do you really want to spend your life swearing at sheep and reps, and smelling of silage?

Does it not worry you that you will become an accomplished liar, and wear the same socks for a fortnight?

Can you cope with a constant stream of big red bills through your letter box, little green aphids eating your wheat and mule yowes that drop dead for no reason known to medical science?

Would you rather plodge about in clarts, wet to the Y-fronts, with a donnered collie dog for company than sit in a warm clean office with a dolly bird secretary and a pension?

You would? You must be stark raving mad, – and that's a very good beginning!

Finding a Farm

The simplest way to acquire a farm is to ensure you have a very rich daddy.

Failing that, the next best bet is a friendly thrice-widowed aunt who has recently become a *late* friendly thrice-widowed aunt and left you all her cash and jewels.

In any case you'll need to find a lot of money from somewhere.

Most likely you will be obliged to arrange a loan similar to the national debt of Brazil just to get started with land, livestock and equipment, somewhere on the dark side of the earth beyond Consett.

However let's assume you *can* lay your hands on a bob or two, have virtually no imagination, and are quite determined to give it a try.

As already explained the supply/demand position in farming is surprisingly out of balance. When a farm *does* become vacant, potential peasants fly in from other planets to look it over, and make hopeful offers to an agent who may well have made his mind up long ago to give the place to his own chinless nephew, fresh out of Cirencester.

Whether it's for sale or rent, it's an auction of sorts, – even if there's no auctioneer with a hammer.

Now obviously you can simply offer more than anybody else in their right mind would offer, – though that may not necessarily impress the seller, who could reckon you're silly, and consequently a poor long-term risk.

...other approach might be to produce that old photograph of the Landlord's mother snogging in the back of a horsebox with the Conservative member for Clartiehole South. This is known as having the 'inside turn'.

The point is, you've got to know the right people and *then* have the right money, – otherwise you've less chance than a snowball in hell.

Of course any old farm won't do. If your dream is of some charming little spot where the grass is always greener and carries 22.4 Friesians to the acre, all squirting out 2,000 gallons, and the barley runs a steady 3½ tonnes without really trying, and massive half-bred yowes all have twins and are never even lame, and all you do is wander about with your faithful old collie, whistling a merry refrain from 'Sound of Music', then I've got news for you bonny lad, – you're in cloud-cuckoo land (or just possibly somewhere in Lincolnshire).

So when searching through the farming press for your 'Shangri-La', beware the over-enthusiastic 'ad'.

'To Let', it says (or For Sale), – The Highly Desirable Holding (sounds a bit like Koo Stark), known as Lower Clartiehole Farm, with all main services, within easy reach of Gateshead, – consisting of Delightful Detached Georgian Farmhouse, Three Modernised Cottages, Extensive Range of Buildings . . . together with 212.37 acres, *or thereabouts* (it always says that, – maybe it's a legal loophole in case somebody measures it all up and discovers only 212.36), of exceptional pasture and arable land.

Sounds pretty good doesn't it? This could be it, – but be careful. The delightful Georgian farmhouse might not have been lived in since George built it in 1700 and something. Modernised cottages might simply mean that the netty has been brought inside from the bottom of the garden, where the fairies were using it. The buildings could be expensive as well as extensive, more suited to a dwarf with a wheelbarrow, than a fore-end loader, – and the 'exceptional' land may be growing nowt but tame wickens and wild oats. And who on earth wants to live within easy reach of Gateshead anyway.

Obviously you must go and check it out, or 'view' as they say in the business. One thing's for sure, you won't be alone, – everybody who's anybody (and a few who aren't), will be there too.

Nobody'll recognise you though, at least not openly, – they might nod quickly with an embarrassed half-smile as they squeeze past in the old byre, – but they won't 'blather on' like they generally do at the mart or the pub.

Instead they'll hurry away to the grain dryer or out into a field of corn, – just a little bit surprised and bothered that you're viewing too.

'What's he doin' here?' they'll be saying, – 'must just be curiosity, I mean he cannot afford t' take a place like this, can he . . .?

'Well y'know what that lot are like,' says his sidekick, – 'gotta know the far end of everythin'.'

But *some* are there to see if it's worth a bid.

Some are there to see if they can *afford* to farm it.

Some are there to see how *badly* the last bloke farmed it.

They prod and poke the land, – how far down will a spade go before it hits clay, or rock, or North Sea gas? They look knowledgeably at bindweed and buttercups, daisies and drains.

They shake the fences, swing the gates, look up and down and along the hemmels and silage pits, trying to conjure up some sort of agricultural equation, the answer to which might pay the landlord, or a bank manager, or both, – and still leave enough to buy the cornflakes and a three-piece suite, and keep going the next year, and the next, and the next.

The womenfolk are there too, – oblivious of the high finance and optimistic arithmetic going on around them. They wander through the farmhouse making world-shattering decisions on whether the deep freeze will fit into the pantry; what colour curtains would suit the living room; will that wardrobe of ours go up the stairs; can I possibly work in a kitchen with such a small window . . .?

While the potential peasant is outside racking his brains how to save a few quid, – they'll be spending money like it was going out of circulation.

'Well the bedroom suite we've got will be no good in here, Alice,' – and as if to justify the proposed new one, – 'and

11

anyway we've had it since before Willie was born y'know, . . . I think it was Mother's actually.'

Her friend won't be listening, she's rebuilding, and changing her lifestyle. 'That fireplace,' she announces, 'it'll have to come out, – and if Charlie thinks he's coming into this kitchen with his wellies on, I've got a surprise for him. I think we'll need a back porch and a downstairs loo as well . . . it's a mess this place isn't it . . . they say she was never at home of course. . . .'

They chatter away, critical hens scratching in the debris of someone else's old nest. Mothers with daughters, wives with sisters, – 'best friends' with 'best friends'.

Meanwhile back in the byre, Charlie (having scratched and gossiped as well) has decided he really hasn't a hope of paying the sort of price everybody else is talking about and, having reached that conclusion, he lights another fag, – quite relieved.

But somebody will come up with the 'necessary', somebody will be confident he can work out a plan of campaign to pay the rent, the rates and the labour, buy a stick, a hammer and a pocket knife, and maybe even support a wife, if he hasn't got one already.

For make no mistake, farming *with* a wife may be difficult enough; without one it's virtually impossible, – well y'gotta have somebody to blame for a start!

'The Other Half'

Pet lamb in the kitchen
puddles on the floor
wellies in the passage
clarts for evermore
barley in the bathroom
straw all up the stairs
worm-drench bottles everywhere
collie castin' hairs
washing done this mornin'
weather forecast fine
friesians in the garden
knickers off the line
here he comes in swearin'
combine bust again
says we could be ruined
and it's comin' on t'rain
kids are home already
telly on the blink
nothin' for the supper
frogspawn in the sink
mother warned her long ago
when she was just sixteen
farmers all have smelly feet
and language quite obscene
the man is just impossible
he rants and raves all day
she'd like to have 'im certified
but who'd take him *away . . .?*

'Colonel and Mrs Carruthers Gore-Blymie of Stately Home, Cheltenham, are pleased to announce the engagement of their daughter Clarissa, to Lt Roger Nigel Nicholas Aubrey Fontelroy, only son of Brigadier and Mrs Waterloo Euston St Pancras Fontelroy, of the Taj Mahal, Pontefract.'

A touch of class there, well-bred, the sort of notice you might find in *Country Life* or the *Tatler*, or the *Daily Telegraph*.

Meanwhile in the *Huddersfield Herald* we might see . . .

'Mr & Mrs Joe Crabtree of 112a Mafeking Gardens, announce the engagement of their youngest daughter Edith, to Alf Batt, 14th son of the late Bernie Batt and Mrs Ethel Batt of 823 Railway Street' . . . and not a moment too soon probably.

You see the difference, don't you? I mean you seldom have a Nigel Nicholas from Cheltenham marrying an Edith from Mafeking Gardens, Huddersfield, – not if it can be avoided anyway.

It can happen of course, the odd belted Earl *does* occasionally run off with the stripper from Broomhill Social Club, and a lovely couple they make, might even live happily ever after, and all that stuff, – but generally the various sections of society tend to stick together.

Obviously there's going to be a bit of friction if Clarissa wants to get tarted up for the Hunt Ball, while husband Alf fancies a skinful of Federation Special and a game of darts 'doon the club'.

It's always been this way, and nowhere is it more apparent than in the world of the peasant. He more than most must choose his spouse with caution.

And she should have a long hard look at the prospects as well.

Any marriage manual or romantic novel she may have read, any evidence from blissful townie brides, any advice from the back pages of *Woman's Own* or Marjorie Proops, – are all irrelevant. There is no reliable reference book for the potential peasant's wife. No one who has gone before has dared to write about it, – and nobody would believe them anyway.

14

The primary difference that sets the farming husband apart is the nature of his job of course, – which in turn affects his lifestyle and his behaviour.

Mr 'Average Townie' wakes up in the morning, folds back the duck-down duvet, strolls across the landing, past the radiator, to the bathroom. He washes, shaves, gets dressed, has his breakfast, kisses the wife and kids goodbye, and catches the 8.15 to the office, with *The Times* tucked underneath his arm.

On the other side of the city, another fella is doing more or less the same thing, except he maybe catches a bus to the factory, with a bait tin and the *Sun* tucked underneath his bomber jacket.

The point is they both vanish for the rest of the day. They come home at night of course, sometimes with a pay packet.

The weekend is their own, – take the family to the zoo, the wife out for an 'Indian', an evening with the lads maybe. It's all cut and dried, neat 'n' tidy, nine t'five, with a bath on Friday, and a pension when you're knackered.

But it's not like that with Sep the peasant.

For a start he doesn't wake up and wander to the bathroom in the morning. Chances are he hasn't been to sleep, that's why. Most peasants spend at least some of the night thrashing about the bed, doing whatever job they've been concerned with the day before, or hope to do tomorrow, – they just can't 'turn off'.

If Sep has been stacking straw bales all day, he stacks straw bales all night as well. He whips his wife's pillow out from under her and stacks it on top of his, – then whips his pillow out and stacks it on top of hers. And so on, – and so on, – all night, – until they get up, exhausted.

It's even worse if he's been clipping sheep, – he has the nightie off her half a dozen times, and wrapped up!

No, our hero won't get washed and shaved and trundle off to work in a clean suit, and he won't kiss the wife and kids goodbye either.

Morning finds him leaping straight into his wellies (strategically placed to save time, and still steaming gently from yesterday). He'll have had a cup of tea, a fag, and been to the loo before Terry Wogan has cracked his first joke. It's not that he's alert and rarin' to go, – it's just necessary to get up and get out, and deal with the inevitable disasters as quickly as possible, – and the sooner you get it over with, the better.

Later on breakfast will be like a commemoration service for the dead of two world wars. To speak is obscene, to laugh can be terminal.

The only sounds will be of food going down, and the apprehensive whispering of nervous children leaving hurriedly for the comparative safety of the school-room.

Fortunately as the day progresses and some semblance of order is achieved among the chaos outside, his manner may improve a little. He may even say something when he comes in for coffee.

Don't expect too much though, – it's unlikely he'll break into a chorus from the 'Student Prince', or quote from the works of Omar Khayyám.

If you're lucky it might be some little gem like, 'I've injected that bloody yow fourteen times this week, and there she is this mornin' lyin' upside down!'

Now ladies should be warned that just because *he* speaks, there is no reason for her to join in, certainly not so early in the day. And for God's sake don't come up with a question about that sick yow, such as, 'is she dead, dear?' – or 'what was the matter with it, pet?' Such apparently uncomplicated questions could disturb the man considerably, – and there *is* the possibility that you might join the yow.

Not to worry though, – he'll be back in for lunch (called dinner in farming circles), – and you may get a chat then. Don't push it though, especially if you've heard him on the phone to a mechanic or a vet, – that means trouble.

He might go off to the mart in the afternoon, in which case this is the nearest he'll get to smart business gear. He will probably change his cap and wash his wellies under the outside tap.

He's back for tea of course, and if he bought nowt at the mart, he'll be full of derision for those who did. If on the other hand he purchased a wagon-load of Hereford bullocks, he'll attempt to convince himself, his wife and children and the dog that only Hereford bullocks were worth the money today.

You see missus, you've got to put up with the professional peasant all day and every day. None of this off to work, 'see you at six, darling', stuff. He's there or thereabouts all the time, scruffy, smelly, and whether you like it or not, – devoted first and foremost to the well-being of Clartiehole Farm.

You could come second, but don't bank on it, – depends how good a collie dog he's got.

Comes the weekend when the nice clean cars, filled with nice clean families, crawl out into the countryside or down to the coast, when couples sit sipping a drink or two in a friendly pub on a Saturday night, or chat merrily over afternoon tea in a country hotel on Sunday, – when we all go off to see granny, or . . . you can forget all that sort of thing, pet, he'll not move.

Well the lambin's not finished yet is it? Or the corn's not sown, or a heifer's calved, or the pigeons are eating his rape, – or he's asleep.

By no stretch of the imagination is he a 'romantic', your English peasant, – so don't expect second honeymoons (you can't be *too* sure about the first one). Don't expect soft lights and violins, or candle-lit suppers at Luigi's, playing footsie under the table. There'll not be a lot of classy dinner parties like you see on telly, with suave elegant gentlemen and seductively gowned ladies eating After Eight Mints, and knocking back the odd bottle of fine old Claret, discussing holidays in the Seychelles.

It's just not like that down on the farm, – after supper (dinner to the rest of the world), – he's knackered, poor auld git. All he wants to do is watch the football and kip. In fact you'll probably have to wake 'im up to get him to bed, – the sex-crazed fool that he is.

In fact while we're on the subject, the peasant's entire love life will probably have been a fairly subdued affair right from those first bewildered adolescent stirrings in a bus shelter after school.

Perhaps it's because young Sep, and others like him, see creation, life, basic biology, every day, – the bull in the back field, the sow farrowing, the yow lambing, the tup with his top lip curled. (I remember one of our kids asking his mother if I wore a sire-sign harness in bed.) Maybe all that tends to dilute the romance.

Still Sep will have his courting moments of course, – he'll have as many hormones as anyone else, and probably a Ford van with an old wool-sack in the back as well.

Fair enough he probably won't walk hand in hand through meadows green, without commenting on the apparent lack of S.26 British Certified Cocksfoot in the sward beneath his true love's feet. He may well snuggle up in the back row of the Odeon, but almost certainly feel obliged to express some concern at the poor finish on the second thigh of those Texas Longhorns that John Wayne is driving through the canyon.

18

His enormous feet, swollen by rain and clarts will over-whelm demure maidens at village dances, and his vast rustic hands will create confusion even among more worldly females, who reckon they've seen everything, – and have!

His urban cousins will only venture out secure in the knowledge they look and smell irresistible, – they may even have a bath! But young Sep, depending on the importance of the occasion, may not change at all, and that subtle something that draws everyone's attention as the evening warms up could well turn out to be a broken bottle of lamb dysentery serum in his combat jacket pocket.

Obviously the woman in his life has to be special, or at least different. Where others might turn away in the face of such rampant apathy she must be prepared to hang on, rejoicing in the challenge to change him from what he's happy to be into what she thinks she'd be happier with. No chance.

That's the picture, ladies, – perhaps you'd rather settle for a little semi in suburbia with 'Chez-nous' on the garden

gate, ducks clinging to the living room wall, coffee mornings and a supermarket round the corner.

But if you're as daft as a brush, you *can* have a big draughty house in the country, – it'll probably be full of kids, pet lambs, wellies, obscenities, clarts and sticky half-empty worm drench tins . . . though you certainly can't expect it to be that good all the time of course.

From the male point of view – the ordinary peasant's view – the rules are simple.

It's just no good picking some scatter-brained bird from Chelsea or Jesmond and expecting her to survive the slings and arrows of outrageous agriculture for more than twenty minutes. It doesn't matter how much you fancy 'er, – it won't work. (There are exceptions of course, – but it takes an extraordinary townie woman to cope with a peasant's lot.)

Oh, she'll probably be keen enough to try, 'cos she'll have this silly technicolour fantasy of fragrant clover and giddy lolloping lambs skipping through the fields, with her sweet self in tight jeans and a checked shirt ministering to your every need, as she helps pioneer a heavenly little plot from nature's vast wilderness.

Her mother might be even keener (depends on what you've been up to), – she'll have a similar mixed-up vision of a tweedy pipe-smoking gentleman, impressing the neighbours as he drives up in a Range-Rover at weekends.

They're both mad, – get out of there as soon as it's dark, seek political asylum somewhere if necessary.

Realistically you've got to find someone who has a fair idea what lies in store, and is still silly enough to have a go.

Someone who's seen and heard father screaming at dogs, sheep and mother, – and can still smile about it (weakly perhaps, but smile nevertheless).

Someone who at an early age came into close contact with a three-week-old wellie sock, a shirt tail used to clean plugs, someone who can recognise the pain in a man's eyes as he discovers the phone's out of order when the combine's conked out, or when a calf's kicked him in the 'goolies'.

Someone who can tell a persistent rep where he should go to, – and persuade another that there's a cheque in the post and hang on to yet another, filling him full of coffee until the boss gets back.

Such creatures are as rare as midges in a frost, in fact there might soon be a world shortage.

What's that? . . . Did I hear some female reader mutter something about 'male chauvinist pig'?

There's one to avoid for a start, she'll be no good. Well, – what does she expect, – sheep *and* sympathy, overdrafts *and* understanding . . .?

Such expectations from the so-called 'fairer sex' can lead to nothing but trouble, so to end this chapter let us briefly consider the case of great uncle Herbert, – it may serve as a warning to the over-enthusiastic liberation lobby.

Now old Herbert was a perfectly normal hard-working conscientious peasant, who, to his everlasting bewilderment, came up before Judge Hymie Greenblatt, charged with unreasonable behaviour towards his wife Ada.

'Is is true,' asked the Judge, 'that on the 14th of March last year, you did assault your wife, causing her to seek refuge inside a wuffler 'til after dark?'

'That's right yer honour,' said Herbert.

'Tell me about it,' said the Judge, 'and remember Herbert you are under oath.'

'Well yer honour, Sir,' said Herbert, 'Y'see I'd been tryin' all day to set this brainless triplet who wouldn't suck on to a totally donnered mule gimmer who kept knockin' the lamb and me all over the byre floor, when in walks Ada. "Why are you sittin' there on the byre floor doin' nothin'," she says; "your supper's gettin' cold, – and why is that gimmer's nose bleeding?" . . . so I threw a shovel at 'er!'

'Is that all?' asked Judge Hymie.

'Well no,' said Herbert, 'I threw a broom at 'er as well, and a pail, and bale of straw . . . and the mule gimmer.'

'I see,' said the Judge. 'The prosecution also alleges that on June 20th you did threaten your wife with a length of rope, – what have you got to say to that?'

'I can't deny it, yer honour, but I was sore provoked.'

'Go on.'

'Y'see we'd been trying to make some hay for a fortnight, the weather was unsettled, showers every other day, – and we still had twenty acres lying. Eventually on the Monday we had it nearly perfect . . . got the baler ready and went once up the field, then the heavens opened up again. We were all soaked and foamin', and when I went into the house to get changed, there she was all upset about her bloody washin' on the line. She went on and on about two pairs of knickers and a string vest that were still out there, wet, – and how she'd never get the ironing done . . . I couldn't stand it any more yer honour, so I pulled the clothes line down and wrapped it round her neck. I would've strung her up as well, but the postman came with a subsidy cheque, so I cooled down a bit.'

The Judge listened to all this very carefully, 'I think it could be argued,' he said, 'that you have shown considerable restraint, Herbert. However, you must realise that women

22

have a completely different sense of values, and they are altogether gentler, more fragile creatures . . .'

'He's a rotten pig,' screamed Ada from the gallery, 'he should be shot and hanged and put in prison!'

'Order madam, please,' said the patient Judge Hymie; 'we must move on to the final allegation in this disturbing case.' He looked down at his notes. 'The prosecution claims that on September 3rd you ran over your wife with a combine harvester. This is quite serious, Herbert, were you perhaps drunk in charge of the machine?'

'No, yer honour, of course not, and anyway I just ran over her foot. Y'see the damn machine went on fire, belchin' smoke it was, the belts all melted, the drum bunged up solid, the cutter bar wouldn't come off the ground and the barley was all blowin' over the back. It was a disaster, – there we were running around frantic, when she drives calmly into the field all tarted up for a coffee mornin' at Hilda's and says, "Why aren't you combining today, dear? . . . Willie Thompson up the road has finished his harvest already . . . is the combine broken?" '

'Good Lord,' exclaimed Judge Greenblatt, 'is this true?'

'I swear it yer honour,' said Herbert.

'Case dismissed!' said the Judge.

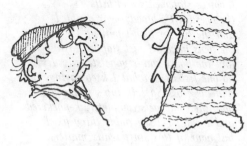

23

What Kind of Farmer?

The wheat has a touch of the eye spot
and a dash of Septoria too
the yowes are all riddled with footrot
and the VAT man is threatening t' sue
the dipper is quietly leaking
and I think I've run over the cat
and the rest of the family aren't speaking
but there's nothing unusual in that
the old septic tank's overflowing
the tame oats have wild ones as well
wickens the only thing growing
and right now I've nothing t' sell
there's a townie been digging m' taties
and the rent's going up so I'm told
and the pigeons are nibbling m' bagies
and Sweep's chasing cars on the road
every morning the postie brings trouble
invoices statements and bills
the overdraft's bloody near doubled
and the tractor won't pull up the hill
the hens have all just stopped laying
and the house cow's gone steadily dry
no one listens to what I keep saying
and the cross Suffolk tup's gonna die
now the combine's completely k-nackered
and I can't get the ruddy thing fixed
but none of this stuff really matters
luck and farming have always been mixed . . .

To a large extent the farm you acquire will determine what line you're going to take, – the size of it, the soil and so on and, as already mentioned, how much lolly you can lay your hands on.

The Ministry of Agriculture will simply give you a number to keep their computers happy, but most other interested parties tend to class us as 'dairy farmers', 'mainly arable', or 'hill farmers', and so on.

The type of farm and the style of farming will also determine how much work you will do. The eternal myth that all farmers leap out of their sack long before dawn breaks and flog themselves non-stop through the day till well after dark is a useful story when discussing the merits of subsidies with townies, – but it's seldom a proper picture. Anybody who works that hard, all the time, is probably so inefficient he's doing everything twice.

However, some farming styles *do* require more effort than others, – and some thought should be given to the type of peasant you want to be.

Dairy Farmer?

Well a regular milk cheque always comes in handy and it's the nearest you'll get to anything resembling a wage packet, – but who in his right mind wants to extract milk from a bunch of dozy old cows twice a day for life?

It doesn't stop flowing on Sundays and Christmas Day y'know. Doesn't matter how technical and silicone-chipped your parlour is, – those cows have gotta be 'relieved' fourteen times a week, fifty-two weeks a year. It goes on and on, and on, – like 'Coronation Street'.

Arable Farming?

This has become very fashionable since World War II, – so much so that the patchwork of barley, wheat and yellow rape stretches further and higher than ever before.

Arguably you won't have to work quite so hard or so often in this line of agriculture, – but you *are* at the mercy of mother nature more than most (and she can be an awkward moody bitch). It's not easy to be amusing when you're combining soggy wheat at a moisture content of 30 per cent, – or a field of barley, most of which blew out the night before.

Furthermore many grain merchants are directly descended from Sicilian bandits, and make second-hand car dealers look like novice monks.

They have concocted special rules for the grain trade which ensure that if there's a can to carry, – the grower will 'volunteer' to carry it. He sows the stuff, sprays it, fertilises it, sprays it again, harvests it, dries it and eventually sends the culmination of a year's work and worry off to the miller, the brewer, or whoever.

Instead of a cheque, he may well receive a telephone call informing him that the whole lot's been rejected at the mill (five minutes before they were due to stop for tea), because somebody found a dead beetle in the bottom of a 20-ton wagon.

By the time this startling discovery is relayed to the 'disappointed' peasant the mill has closed for the weekend, the merchant is sobbing sympathetically into his pint at the Conservative club and the haulier is wondering where he can dump this 'foul disease-ridden load'.

In the cereal business, it is dangerous to count your chickens *after* they're hatched.

Hill Farming?
Hill farmers are a special breed and deserve a chapter to themselves, possibly even a film, – or a video nasty.

Briefly though, to be an ideal hill farmer you should be a big strong lad with a red face, hands like shovels, feet like amphibious landing craft, carry a fancy stick wherever you go, wear 'glazie-leggins' all the time, and be naturally addicted to sheep.

The job, as you can imagine, is lonely. Your closest friend is likely to be called Spot or Sweep, – and I don't have to tell you what a lifetime's association with a horde of 'Blackie' yowes can do to the mind.

Mixed?

Most farmers are classed as 'mixed'. Obviously this label tends to be less prestigious than some others (such as 'barley baron'), and often leaves the townie confused and the eager young 'rep' unimpressed. Their preconceived notions of a 'beef breeder', 'sheep farmer' or even a 'chicken rearer', are easier to understand.

Well imagine, for example, if some delicious little débutante starts chatting you up at a party and asks you what you do for a living. If all you can say is, 'Well, er, I'm a mixed farmer . . .' – not only is she likely to be doubtful about your parentage, she may be suspicious about your 'credentials' as well.

There is a simple way round this problem, however. The rule is never to commit yourself to any particular type of farming, – not immediately anyway.

When she flutters her eyelashes, or whatever, and asks '. . . and what do *you* do sweetie?', – you reply in a casual, almost bored manner, 'What? – oh, I farm actually. . . .'

'Ooo,' she'll twitter, with a bit o'luck, 'how fascinating . . . and do you have cows and bulls and hens and things . . .?'

At this point it's plain to see you can give her any spiel you fancy, – she's obviously as thick as a plank as far as agriculture's concerned (didn't I tell you that townies know nowt about farming . . .?).

'Ah well you see my dear,' you croon in your best CLA voice, 'it's what we call a mixed farm' (you can say that now); 'yes, we have hens' (so it's only two Rhode Island Reds and a bantie cock, but what does she know), 'and cattle of course, and yes a few sheep . . . can I get you another gin 'n' tonic? . . . and by the way my name's . . .'

Anyway enough of that, – where were we? Oh yes, we were discussing what type of farmer you might be. . . .

Well it's not all that important really. 'Mixed' is as good as any, – probably more interesting. All your eggs are not in one big fragile basket (they're in several small fragile baskets), – and if you're brighter than the average brick, have a crooked accountant, a friendly bank manager, a

27

brother-in-law who happens to be the local tax inspector, a numbered account in the Cayman Islands, and a string of bingo halls in your wife's name, you might just manage to scrape some sort of living out of it all, – if the weather's reasonable.

Sale

See that man with gambler's eye
pencil notebook fancy tie
lookin' for a canny buy
and money in his pocket . . .
any sale on any day
cold December sunny May
right t' the very end he'll stay
in search of instant profit . . .
tired tup and toothless yow
baldy hen arthritic cow
he knows where and when and how
to make a fiver off it . . .

The farm you have acquired is almost as old as the world itself, – well perhaps hardly *that* old, but for sure somebody had it long before you came along, – and whether he's gone off to that great green pasture in the sky, or simply to a bungalow in Berwick, – there will be a sale before you can take over.

The following then, is an eye-witness account by the agricultural correspondent of the *Clartiehole and District Gazette*, of a typical farm sale, – which should give the new prospective peasant some idea of what to expect on the day.

The rural community has a nose for farm sales, he writes, – and I just followed the pick-ups and Land-Rovers and dirty cars. The only other indication that something was 'on', was a piece of damp cardboard nailed to a telegraph pole, with an arrow pointing down a bye-road, with 'To the Sale' scrawled in capital letters.

A thirty-acre rig and furrow car park was already pretty

full, and it was beginning to rain. I parked near the gate and followed the crowd over the field towards the farm buildings.

'I thought farmers were supposed t'be hard up,' grunted some character who should've known better, 'half the bloody county's here!' He slammed the door of his new Mercedes and strode away to the action.

The bloke parked next to him tried to pretend the battered 'J' reg. Mini pick-up with no silencer wasn't really his, and hurried after him.

The auctioneer had already started to sell the long lines of 'machinery'. I recalled that in the advert the machinery had been described as 'well-maintained'. No indication had been given of how *long* it had been 'well-maintained'.

You would imagine that the demand for horse-drawn scarifiers, and a beer crate full of congealed 'wonder' cattle medicines might be rather limited now, – but everything got a bid.

An old 'acrobat' hay turner with about as many teeth as a seventeen-crop mule made new price, and so did a corn drill seized as tight as a duck's backside with last year's fertiliser.

A thistlecutter cunningly camouflaged by generations of hen muck was in great demand, a collection of spades and shovels worn down to the size of dessert-spoons, a one-pronged fork, a two-legged milking stool, a forty-gallon drum of creosote and a length of rusty chain, made a fortune.

'Always needed a good chain, gotta pull the bloody tractor every morning to start it,' declared the embarrassed buyer, as everyone turned to stare at him in astonishment. 'It's a right good chain that is,' he went on, looking for someone to justify his purchase, – 'pull anything that chain will.' But they'd all moved on to the next lot.

'Now this is in perfect order,' shouted the auctioneer as he bustled his way through to the tractor and banged his stick busily on the front tyre, 'Done virtually nowt, this machine,' he said. 'Start her up 'Arry.'

'Arry the clerk (who also acted as assistant auctioneer and cattle drover), put down his book of figures, leapt enthusiastically onto the damp tractor seat and turned the key.

He fiddled with the gear handle and turned the key.

He muttered some obscenities and turned the key.

He was about to kick it (and turn the key), when the auctioneer saved him: 'Never mind, 'Arry, it was working perfectly well this morning, – we'll sell her as she stands . . . do I hear a thousand? . . . eight hundred then, anybody will . . . five hundred, surely gentlemen?' – and a 'gentleman' in suede shoes and a maroon cardigan looked him straight in the eye and without moving his lips said, 'fifty quid.'

The auctioneer appeared to be insulted, but began the long weary haul to justify his commission. Long before he reached five hundred pounds, 'suede shoes' had retired to the beer tent.

'Sheep next,' shouted the auctioneer, and strode off purposefully to the ring of hurdles and wire netting.

A big fat important dealer from Yorkshire climbed into the ring, as big fat important dealers tend to do (so that everyone can see just how big and important they really are), – but he caught his foot in the wire netting, and most of the ring fell down.

Everybody laughed like a drain.

'Now these sheep haven't been abused in any way,' said the auctioneer using the language peculiar to this sort of occasion (see Glossary) . . . 'they'll shift anywhere. . . . Now gentlemen what am I bid for the first pen, – three-crop they are, and all twins. How about a hundred, alright then seventy-five and start 'em . . . I can't accept any less. . . .' But he did, and at fifty the big fat important dealer eased the weight of his sprained ankle and winked a confidential bid.

'Hellova trade,' said a bloke in a fore 'n' aft hat, 'stone-mad those sheep, – half of them's got orf y'know, . . . did y' see that, – orf, terrible thing orf!'

'Really?' spluttered a little man in a full-length ex-army greatcoat, who'd bought two lots, – and he hurried away feeling sick, and wondering how on earth you cured orf.

'Stand on!' screamed the auctioneer, he was getting a 'flier' now, and he could see his 'cut' piling up already.

The Mercedes man bought nearly all the cattle at prices that made people mumble to each other.

'Hellova trade,' said fore 'n' aft, 'stone-mad those cattle . . . half of them's got husk y'know . . . did y'see that? – husk, – terrible thing husk!'

'Makes you wonder where he gets the money,' grinned a very polite and well-dressed rep., who'd been following a potential combine buyer around all day, like a labrador.

'Money!' exclaimed the potential combine buyer, 'he's got no money, – it's all *hers* y'know, – he married it, that's what *he* did . . . no fool that man.'

'Suede shoes' was telling dirty jokes in the beer tent, surrounded by shiny-faced young farmers.

'Ex-army greatcoat' was frantically arranging transport to get his diseased sheep away home and out of sight.

'Arry, still foaming about the reluctant tractor, was busy collecting cheques, and 'doing the books', – he'd be there for hours yet.

The auctioneer poured himself another large whisky to ease his sore throat.

The car park was beginning to look like a 'turnip break' as the 'J' reg. Mini pick-up slithered out onto the road and made for home, with a tup in the back.

Mercedes was screaming for someone to give him a push out of the rig-bottom. No one seemed to hear, – except the very polite and well-dressed rep.

'You got some very nice cattle today,' he grinned eagerly. . . .

What You'll Need to Get Started

Gone the horse
the pikes of hay
gone the stooks and stacks
the draining spade
the scythe the rake
and sixteen stones on aching backs
gone the cart
the load of muck
a pole a perch a chain
the turnip knife
the belly band
and cutting thistles in the rain
gone the bus
the village school
gone the threshing day
the railway sacks
the singled drill
and flitting in the month of May
combine now
and big round bales
sealed in plastic bags
intervention
conservation
music plays in tractor cabs . . .

This chapter can be neatly divided into three parts.

There's your 'fixed equipment', which sooner or later will rattle loose; what's known as 'dead stock' which, when it doesn't function properly, you will undoubtedly treat as if it were alive; and of course there's livestock, – and the more you have of that, the more you'll have stone dead.

Fixed Equipment

This includes such things as storage bins, grain dryer, perhaps a mill for grinding barley meal, – anything in fact that is 'fixed' to the spot.

It is advisable to have as little of this stuff as possible because it tends to disintegrate just when you need it most.

This naturally pleases electricians and mechanics in the neighbourhood, who you will need to repair it, generally at a weekend, or at least after five o'clock on exorbitant hourly rates of overtime. It will also please the dealer, who sees the opportunity to sell you the 'new improved model'.

It's no good trying to be a 'do-it-yourself' man. For one thing you'll have to keep a mountainous supply of nuts and bolts, – and you'll just waste time discovering that none of the nuts fits any of the bolts. You'll also need an arsenal of spanners, wrenches and socket sets, all of which will be either just too big or just too small. In any case they inevitably get lost, – along with the skin from your knuckles.

What's more you'll seldom have time to do the job completely, – because you'll no sooner get the offending machine dismantled, than a randy heifer will have to be taken to the bull, or your mother-in-law will have to be taken to the bus.

By the time you get back to the job, the kids will have made a Dalek out of the bits left lying around.

Better by far to rely on the simple technique taught me by my father who when any machine broke down would kick it, blame my mother, and then limp to the telephone for a mechanic.

Only two tools are required on a well-organised farm even in this technological age: a durable claw hammer, preferably coloured bright red so you can find it again after you've thrown it away in a bad fettle, and a spade (see sheep).

Dead Stock

Like the afore-mentioned fixed equipment, dead-stock should be kept to the absolute minimum. Look at a farmer's hands if you don't believe me, – see how unlike a concert pianist's they are, notice the scars, the black bent nails jammed by fiendish implements. They're all old war wounds suffered in the never-ending battle against fan belts that suddenly slot into place (taking a finger end), rusty nuts that unexpectedly 'give' and fat spanners that slip off thin nuts.

Of course some farms do need some machinery I suppose, like a tractor for instance. The trouble is once you start, it becomes a kind of mechanical diarrhoea, – you can't stop.

Well a tractor by itself isn't much use is it? What y'gonna do with it, – take the wife shopping? (Maybe that's not a bad idea actually, – a few draughty trips to the supermarket riding on the mudguard might save you a bob or two), – but to be realistic you'll probably buy a plough instead.

A plough eh? – fair enough, but what happens to all this land after you've turned it over? That's right, – you *cultivate* it don't you, you *disc* it, you *harrow* it, you *roll* it (the shed's filling up already). And then you sow a crop with a fancy drill, you spray it with a space-age sprayer, 'top-dress' it with a new 'spinner'. That tractor's fully employed now, isn't it, – in fact you'll need another one to drag all this gear about. And we haven't even discussed cutting silage, baling hay, combining at harvest time or shifting mountains of muck. . . .

Anyway you see what I mean, if you're not careful, you can end up with a million quids worth of technicolour monsters, all neatly oiled and greased, tucked up in their own asbestos dolls' house, and most of the year they're dormant, like a grizzly bear or your member of Parliament.

Twice around the field and they're worth half what you paid for them, – three times around, and the eager dealer is back with an unrepeatable trade-in offer, four times around and you hit a boulder. . . .

Livestock
It seems that in my long, undistinguished career as a peasant I have achieved a certain modest notoriety as a cynic when discussing various forms of agricultural livestock.

The fact remains that anyone who imagines that all farm animals are born on a bright spring morning to the sound of the Ebchester and District Ladies Choral Society's rendering of 'Ave Maria', go on to mature and eventually end up at the mart, happy in the knowledge that they have left their owner lots of money, – has been drinking too much 'Newcastle Brown'.

The equation is very straightforward: the more animals you keep, – the more are likely to expire.

Nevertheless we will consider in detail some of the animals the peasant may wish to bring onto his farm.

Sheep

The yow is a truly remarkable beast
that man's been unable to tame
she would never be caught if God hadn't thought
to make most of the stupid things lame . . .
the auld yow is born a peculiar beast
she defies mother nature's great plan
no creature on earth has ambition at birth
to drop dead just as soon as she can . . .
the yow is a thoroughly awkward beast
from her lugs to the tip of her tail
two tits and a tooth and t' tell you the truth
a brain like a mouldy straw bale . . .!

If at all possible sheep should *not* be included in your farm plan. Several enlightened advisors have in fact come to the conclusion that they should be abolished along with sago and flying pickets.

However, let us look at some of the hazards and misunderstandings associated with this extraordinary creature.

I will not waste time describing the various breeds, basically there's not a lot of difference between any of them. They may look different of course. Obviously the Half-bred is much bigger and heavier than the Swaledale; some will have horns and the type of fleece will vary as well, though it will all come out in handfuls when you try to catch any of them. In all cases it is quite safe to say their behaviour pattern is similar to that of a demented budgie, and designed primarily to drive the shepherd insane.

Their life's ambition is to wake up dead.

For example you may imagine, reasonably enough, that

because there's four feet of snow on the ground and nothing remotely edible in sight, they'd all appreciate a few crushed oats in a trough, or a bale of sweet-smelling hay in a heck. Well naturally most of them will of course, but you will be surprised to discover that several of the leaner, hungrier ones (the most needy cases), will 'tek the huff'.

This is not as far as I know a notifiable disease, but it's fatal nevertheless. The symptoms are a stubborn refusal to eat anything, followed in a few days by collapse into the nearest wet hole.

One of the most common disorders among sheep is 'footrot'. This is a particularly nasty infection between the hooves (rather like the symptoms associated with continuous wearing of nylon socks), – and unless treated quickly, it will render the animal lame and force her to walk on her knees. These in turn become infected with knee rot, which renders her not only lame, but very halt as well.

It is worth noting also that sheep are life-long members of the 'worm benevolent society', and as such do everything in their power to provide a suitable comfy home for all species of parasitic organisms, from ticks to nematodirus. A sheep is actually a worm in sheep's clothing! (Not many people know that.)

But it's at lambing time that the yow will strain to the limit the resources of medical science, animal husbandry and one's wavering faith in the Almighty.

This is the time for 'staggers', for 'the sickness', for a sudden lack of magnesium, or calcium, copper, cobalt, or any one of a hundred obscure trace elements, which until recently no one had ever heard of.

It is the time when the weather is traditionally at its worst. Lambing under cover obviously gives much more protection, but even then it is essential to sit and watch every move throughout the night, otherwise chaos can be the order for the following day.

It is not uncommon to leave a settled quiet flock at midnight, and at two in the morning discover one over-enthusiastic old mule ewe claiming to have given birth to five threes, seven pairs and a massive single, when in fact she hasn't even lambed at all.

Firstly then a few tips for the lambing season.

Contrary to most learned works on the subject, I believe it to be inadvisable to feed the pregnant ewe more than the absolute minimum for survival. This enables you to achieve the desired emaciated flock which, when the necessity arises, you'll find much easier to catch. (A word of warning here, – it can be dangerous at this stage to make a noise like a bale of hay, as you will run the risk of being overwhelmed before you can climb out over the gate.)

Which brings us to the lambing field itself.

Naturally, this should be well fenced with strong posts no more than, say, a foot apart, together with perhaps seventeen strands of barbed wire, and pig netting to a height of approximately eight feet.

Avoid at all costs the time-wasting practice of erecting straw-bale shelters, because you will find that on a particularly stormy night the ewes will either lie on the windward side and perish, or eat the straw bales, – and then perish.

It is imperative that the new shepherd fully understands the ewe's attitude at this time. Her first priority is of course to die, and failing that she believes her only real hope for salvation in the hereafter is to ensure that the shepherd dies, – or at least becomes a gibbering wreck estranged from his wife and family.

Extreme care must be taken when the ewe actually gives birth to her offspring. One must remember that sheep are unable to count accurately above nought, – consequently although on occasions she may be aware of motherhood, she will be unsure as to what extent, and could well abandon one or all of her lambs, pretending she was elsewhere at the time. She may just as readily, as already indicated, claim everybody else's.

To eliminate this frustrating experience some older and wiser shepherds use a technique passed down through generations of half-crazed hillmen. This consists simply of a vicious blow between the ewe's lugs with a stout net-stake.

The practice is also very useful when 'setting-on' the orphan lamb. More often than not, the ewe, elated at having lost her own young ones, refuses to be lumbered with somebody else's hungry brat, but her mind (I use the word advisedly), can be 'changed', if she is first rendered semi-conscious by the above-mentioned lambing aid. Golf enthusiasts have discovered that a 7 iron has a similar effect.

Attention should also be drawn to the farmer or shepherd from 'up the road', who year after year claims to have had the best lambing he can remember.

'Never lost a sheep,' he'll tell you, as you bury another one of yours. 'Just over two hundred per cent again,' he'll say. 'Mind you,' he moves closer as if to divulge some sordid secret about the vicar; 'mind you, our yowes were tremendous fit, never had them better . . .' he goes on and on.

Some consolation can be gained from this traumatic encounter, however. Look carefully into his eyes, and you'll see that he's got that vacant expression of someone who is deranged.

He is.

However for those who remain blindly convinced that sheep *must* be part of their farming enterprise and life-style, some further advice on how to get a flock started may be useful.

First then go to a mart and buy some ewes. The breed is largely immaterial, though perhaps it should be pointed out that big soft Suffolks do find it hard to survive on a heathery mountain, and Scottish Blackfaces often get rampant indigestion when exposed to green grass 'doon bye'.

For your first visit to a sheep sale you must carefully disguise yourself either as an impoverished idiot, recently released from an old Shepherds Rest Home, or as a dealer from York-shire, otherwise you will certainly be taken for a ride.

Even then you will inevitably end up with a couple of sheep who are stone blind, several consumed with footrot, eight with one tit, and a few broken-mouthed 'chasers', – all described by the auctioneer as 'grand shiftin' gimmers off high ground.'

When you get them home your primary problem will be to keep them there. It is not generally understood that sheep, like pigeons, are often equipped with a 'homing device'. One unscrupulous shepherd in the Alwinton area recently confessed to having sold the same batch of old Blackies for the fifth time in one year.

Obviously the fencing (not only in the lambing field) will have to be checked, especially along boundaries and road-sides, – and any holes should be blocked with old wufflers, vintage zig-zag harrows, and the spring mattress from your granny's brass bed.

Trying to keep the ewes in any one particular field can be difficult. Perhaps the best advice I've come across is to put them into the field *next* to the one you really want them in, – they're bound to creep through sooner or later.

Next, the tup . . . well be warned, that just because you provide your handsome young Suffolk shearling with forty nubile mule maidens to play with, it doesn't ensure he'll stay at home either. He could well abandon them for a posse of pedigree geriatric Jacobs next door, – which may delight the old Jacobs, but is unlikely to impress their owner.

All the recognised literary works on sheep husbandry will advise that you prepare yourself with a wagon-load of syringes, vaccines, serums, sprays, antibiotics, pills, medi-cines and drenches, ancient and modern.

This is a complete waste of time and money, and at best will but delay the inevitable demise of the sick animal. All that is needed, as already indicated, is a good sharp spade.

Collie dogs, often believed by beginners to be an essential part of the shepherd's equipment, are in fact both expensive and unnecessary. But if you insist on having a dog, then you'll have to learn to whistle with your mouth full of fingers, and swear at the same time.

The novice dog handler should stand in an exposed spot, staring enthusiastically into the middle-distance or in the general direction of some sheep and, holding his shepherd's stick in the right hand, shout in a loud clear voice such things as, 'git away bye', or 'hadaway oot', or 'cum inta m'shirt tail here', or 'for god's sake sit doon y'donnered bugger!'

Of course these phrases by no means guarantee that the dog will do anything useful. He could instead be moved to chase a hare or his own tail, or go off with your neighbour's well-bred labrador bitch. But dogs really deserve a chapter to themselves so we'll leave further guidance till later.

Throughout the summer your ewes will be plagued by flies, which, like worms, are attracted to sheep, – and you yourself will be plagued by worm-drench reps, who are attracted to shepherds.

The ewes will all lie on their backs and pretend they can't get up (sometimes they aren't kidding), and the tup will challenge another tup, or a brick wall, to a head-to-head confrontation, and come a poor second.

You will have to clip all your adult sheep of course, probably some time in June (at least those who haven't already lost their wool on brambles and barbed wire, or as a result of some depilating disease), – and this can be hard work.

Films of suntanned Aussies lazily peeling the fleece from a fat doped Merino can be misleading. Most British breeds have fleeces like old fireside mats, stuck tight to the skin to keep out the foul weather. It can be quite an achievement therefore to clip a flock of skinny old native rat bags without also removing a tit and/or both lugs.

However don't be entirely dismayed, – you could end up with a few lambs to sell. This will probably coincide with a ban on exports and a 'World in Action' programme in which a scientific genius with a ginger beard and rimless glasses declares that the latest research indicates that mutton encourages heart attacks.

Well it does of course, – but only when it's alive.

Cattle

Personally I like cattle. They're friendly, they have a capacity to enjoy life, they have an inquisitive sense of humour, – and unlike sheep they generally have 'livability' (in other words they *can* recover from an illness).

The most extraordinary creature I ever bought, was a pot-bellied Friesian who became known as Arthur.

Arthur came in a bunch of young calves bought from a crafty old dealer who must've been thrilled to meet me.

This was the smallest bullock I've ever seen. Riddled with ring-worm, full of obscure bugs and unknown viruses, he looked like a very badly bred whippet.

He should've just quietly died, it would've saved me a lot of bother, – but, as you'll learn, only the good'n's die; the rubbish hang on for ever.

Reasonably enough none of the other calves would have anything to do with such a wreck, and he got knocked about a bit, – so we had to put him into a 'private ward' for special treatment.

Even then he was so small we had to saw the legs of the trough so he could reach the barley meal and good hay we gave him.

But he wouldn't eat that, – instead he ate the trough, the door, a lot of baler twine and an old anorak I left lying about.

You don't need to be a nutritional expert to know that this is not a wholly satisfactory diet for the production of prime British beef, – and sure enough Arthur just looked more ridiculous every day.

The vet came to see him of course, – filled him full of antibiotics and assorted drugs, and went away shaking his head, muttering something about 'bloody miracles'.

At one stage I even considered shooting the animal.

But Arthur somehow survived the winter, and went out to the grass with his big brothers.

He didn't thrive there either, just chewed gates and sucked telegraph poles, until after a couple of wet nights he developed pneumonia, and had to be carried back inside again.

I was sick of the sight of him by now, but naturally nobody would take him off my hands, – I couldn't take him to the mart, wouldn't get a bid, and the auctioneer would probably fall out of his box laughing.

So for another year he went on consuming rubbish and drugs like a four-legged incinerator, until came the next spring I kicked him out once more to take his last chance, – come hell or high water.

It was the high water that got 'im. A week later I found him lying upside down in a wet hole, apparently kicking his last.

'Well that's enough of that,' I thought; we'll get the kennel cart to pick you up in the morning. . . .'

In the morning he was missing.

We found him at dinner time half-way to the pub, happily eating nettles and gravel by the roadside, – and for some reason best known to the patron saint of pot-bellied Friesians, Arthur never looked back after that and grew and grew.

I can't remember just where he ended up, but if anybody recalls a particularly rough steak, with the delicate flavour of baler twine and anorak, – that was probably him.

Anyway back to the broad subject of cattle.

Well you can breed your own of course, in which case you'll need a few heifers and a bull (we'll assume you know why).

Believe it or not though, there are some heifers (and cows) who don't fancy getting pregnant, and some bulls who don't fancy anything. There are cows who haven't any milk and calves who won't suck. It's not as simple as Mother Nature would have you believe.

One thing they all have in common is their ability to eat and eat all the year round. They'll eat grass, hay, wickens, straw, silage, turnips and tractor tyres. You will spend all summer growing food to keep them going all winter, and if you're five minutes late on Christmas morning, they'll be blaring impatiently at the back door.

You *can* dispense with the cows of course, and simply rear bought-in calves on milk substitute, and hope.

In this set-up you really need a controlled environment shed, with individual cubicles for each calf. The design of these pens is critical, – they have to be strong, unpalatable, and narrow enough to prevent the calf turning round. This last requirement is because the diet of a young calf tends to have the same effect as a pailful of prunes, – consequently if they all happen to be facing in the wrong direction as you walk up the alleyway, it can be dangerous.

You can cut a few corners by buying 'stores' and feeding them up for the market, but this too can be fraught with problems. It requires 'mart-sense', and 'black-magic' to buy and sell at the right price, and nobody gets it right *all* the time.

Chances are as soon as you've bought you'll think, 'ye gods that's too much,' – and as if to confirm your worst fears, the auctioneer will appear to be laughing as he shouts out your name for all to hear.

Sure enough as you creep quietly from the ring to have a reassuring look at them in the pen, you'll hear people mumbling such acute observations as, 'they'll never grow y'know,' or 'they've got no backsides,' or the ultimate insult, – 'he must have more money than sense, that bloke!'

In the pen they will appear to have shrunk dramatically since leaving the ring (they have). In fact you might not recognise them until the seller comes along whistling, singing and clapping his hands. He's on his way to buy a new car.

Strangely enough when you're selling, everything changes. The bottom drops out of the trade three minutes before your turn, and everybody goes home. Everybody that is except that dealer from Yorkshire, who snaps them up at twenty quid less than you had them valued at.

What's more, before you can crawl away thoroughly dejected and temporarily ruined, he'll swoop on you from behind, and you'll hear those terrible words, the words that send shudders through the bravest peasant, the sound that spreads despair into the stoutest hearts . . . 'now then young man, you'll have a bit of luck for me I expect. . . .'

That's the store mart; the 'fat' is no better. No sooner are your cattle in prime condition than some enlightened journalist will write an article describing how beef is bad for the complexion, or the government will import vast quantities of frozen hamster from Uganda, or the EEC will just run out of green pounds and the subsidy will melt like snow in a 'fresh'.

In any case the butchers will stand in a huddle by the weighbridge telling dirty jokes and taking turns at buying cattle, so as to keep the trade within *their* reasonable limits.

By this time you will have already discovered that peasants don't do this, – they bid relentlessly against each other, as if the beast in the ring was the last surviving bullock on earth.

Pigs 'n' Hens 'n' Horses

Pigs

There's an old saying that the only part of a pig you can't eat is the squeak.

The pig itself will consume almost everything put in front of it (or behind it for that matter), and convert the intake into meat better than most animals.

High-protein nuts, barley, cabbages, plastic bags and bits of coal, anything goes, – even other pigs, and *your* right leg if you linger too long.

The reason is, I suppose, that pigs begin life in a very competitive atmosphere. They are not like the single calf or the twin lamb, or the solitary helpless foal. Percy the piglet could well be one of fifteen, and if he's not quick off the mark, he could end up very hungry, or very squashed, – especially if mother is a bit excited and only has ten tits.

Nowadays pig keeping is for the specialist, – breeding, feeding, medication and environment have to be of the highest standard for survival in a very competitive and, at the time of writing, totally unsubsidised industry.

Many pork producers would claim theirs is the most efficient way to lose money in farming.

Once upon a time of course every farm had at least one pig who was simply fed on assorted rubbish until he looked like a hippopotamus.

The farmer threw in pailfuls of corn, the wife emptied the dustbin and the vacuum cleaner into the sty, and the kids fed him stale bread and whatever else they didn't like. The old guffie consumed it all, convinced every day was his birthday.

Then just before he actually exploded, the poor fella was

led out into the backyard for the annual ritual slaughter. With a bit of luck it was all over very quickly, and before the day was ended, Percy was potted meat, sausage, spare-ribs and black puddin', – the rest of him 'curing' in the pantry.

Later on the sides were rolled and hung from a beam in the kitchen, where everyone constantly hit their heads on them.

By the time the next pig was ready for the 'chop', the family were all suffering from mild concussion, and pig-sick of thick fat salty bacon for breakfast, dinner and supper.

Now they measure any fat in millimetres with a Geiger counter, – and only produce pigs long and lean. Your grandad may well have lived to be a hundred on home-cured ham and bread 'n' drippin', – but now such a diet is considered as lethal as paraquat.

Hens

And so to hens. All the experts will tell you that the days when you could keep a few friendly speckled old birds scratching about in the backyard, eating tatie-peelin's, tea leaves and crusts are gone forever.

It's uneconomic, they say, inefficient, – the only way to produce eggs is to stuff the unfortunate birds six-deep into a wire cage in a plywood building with no windows, and feed them special pellets at two hundred quid a ton.

It is not entirely without significance that these afore-mentioned experts are invariably employed by the firm that sells the special pellets.

Somewhat like pigs, this can be a quick and efficient way to get poorer.

For a start the plywood building will cost you about the same as a detached villa in Acapulco, and the money needed for the highly complicated equipment to move food in and muck out, to ventilate, fumigate and irrigate the establishment, and generally keep the birds happily squirt-ing out eggs, would keep you in clover for years.

Once you begin producing mountains of eggs every day it's not much use sticking a cardboard sale notice at the farm gate. The only set-up capable of removing your production is either a scruffy Cypriot wholesaler with a string of shops in Wolverhampton or your neighbourhood packing station who, after grading everything very carefully, will give you five pence a dozen less than it cost to get them out of the bird.

If the demand (and the trade), does pick up, this is the time your hens will get fowl pest, coccidiosis or bronchitis, and produce nothing but hen muck. Hen muck has its uses of course, but it can inhibit your social life a bit.

The moral is clear, – the cleverer you are, the more you produce; the more you produce the less you're likely to get for it, – and unless you're the kind of bloke who gambles on the stock market, plays poker every Tuesday night, can steal daffodils from the bishop's garden and sell them to your mother-in-law, – stick with a few friendly speckled old hens scratching about in the backyard. If things get really bad, eat them.

Horses (no farm should be *with* one)
For some inexplicable reason a lot of people seem to think gee-gees are wonderful, man's best friend even.

Perhaps it's got something to do with Clint Eastwood riding off into the sunset or Harvey Smith falling off at Olympia.

The telly is infested with horses, there's racing or show jumping on every day, and a second-rate western on every night.

The countryside's full of them as well. You can't drive to the post office without some redundant Colonel waving you down from the top of a demented gelding.

Although they can appear rather noble creatures, in fact they have a brain almost as small as a politican's, and are similarly unreliable, capable of kicking anybody, or taking a sizeable lump out of your backside when you least expect it.

Contrary to the impression given in movies, they cannot live indefinitely, tied up to a rail outside a saloon. They seldom come when whistled at, and never ever stand still while you climb aboard, let alone fire a '45' between their ears.

Their appetites are enormous, and they chase sheep, chew old ladies' hats, shatter fences and turn your best field into a morass. In short they serve no useful purpose now unless you happen to live in remote parts of Arizona, or west of Hexham, where the internal combusion engine has yet to be seen.

Naturally the 'Hunting Set' will disagree with this analysis, but it should be remembered that these people have fallen off so many times they're more or less 'punchie', and seldom rational.

They can be humoured with such remarks as, 'My word, Rodney, I do believe he's got fetlocks like Arkle,' or 'what superb withers you have, Daphne,' – but they should be actively discouraged from careering all over your farm. This is simply done by either tying all the gates with knotted string at both ends, or shooting the first two riders as they appear over your boundary fence.

50

Dogs

Git away bye m' bonny lad
gan oot gan oot gan wide
y've missed that yow that's lyin' doon
I bet she's been and gone 'n died . . .
come inta me y'brainless hoond
sit doon sit still stay there
I think I saw her blink an eye
ye gods she's lambed a bloody pair . . .
she's up she's off the stupid bitch
gan oot then fetch her here
the lambin' always starts like this
a fortnight early every year . . .

We used to have a dog called Sam, named after an animal who once starred in a bad film.

Our Sam bore no resemblance to the 'actor' however, a massive Alsatian cross wolf who, when required, tore assorted villains to shreds.

Our Sam was a Spanorgi, – a breed seldom seen at Crufts (or anywhere else I suspect), half Spaniel, half Corgi. He was one of a litter of seven, the result of an affair between two pedigree lovers from good homes in Gosforth.

He led a full and active life, devoted almost entirely to the defence of the farm from aerial attack.

As far as I know NATO headquarters never knew that Sam was capable of detecting the approach of fast low-flying aircraft which apparently can foil sophisticated radar. What is perhaps more significant still, having determined from which direction they were coming long before anyone could see or hear them, – he would then chase them off in the opposite direction.

Of course he never actually caught one, and in any case as soon as he figured they were no longer flying over this farm, he lost interest, and came back to prepare for the next intruder foolish enough to violate our airspace.

He developed a fair turn of speed and enormous stamina over the years, especially for a dog with such a ridiculous physique (he had a Spaniel body and Corgi legs), – and there were several well-worn tracks through the garden, down the croft, and into the back field, which accurately traced the flight paths of passing Phantoms and DC 10s.

Sam had no other interests really, except possibly the bitch at the vicarage and the Electricity Board men, one of whom tried to read the meter while we were out and was apparently persuaded not to. We got an assessment that quarter, and a nasty letter about man-eating dogs.

He had no interest in farm livestock, even sheep viewed him with bewildered boredom as he tore past in pursuit of an innocent Boeing.

By evening of course he was knackered and slept soundly under the kichen table.

His successor (dogs don't live for ever either), is a very fat alleged labrador who moves at a speed similar to that of an arthritic seal. She (Meg), could not be persuaded to chase anything faster than a dog biscuit, and if perchance we were ever burgled, would be hard pressed to even bark. She might however lick the villains to death if they lay down on the mat beside her.

Of course, such dogs as these are a liability, – they only eat, sleep and fool around, contributing nothing at all to the desperate struggle for survival in farming.

From an agricultural point of view there are only three types of dog that need be considered (all of them collies), – and they can be classified as follows, – a good dog, a canny dog and a donnered dog.

A good dog is worth his weight in liver-flavoured Kennomeat. He'll follow you to the end of the world, suffer any hardship, unlimited abuse and still be devoted to you. We'll come back to him in a minute.

Dogs

A donnered dog should be either shot at an early age or abandoned somewhere in Brixton, otherwise he'll just drive you insane. He'll probably look smashin', – gleaming coat, sparkling eyes, picture of canine competence, – but he'll sleep all day, out of sight somewhere, pretend to be deaf and earn a reputation as a sex-maniac after innumerable clandestine associations with every terrier and lurcher for miles around. He might well be afraid of sheep.

At least you soon know where you stand with him, – but a *canny dog* is the worst of all, – he'll be totally inconsistent.

'Git away bye,' you'll shout on Monday morning, and off he'll go like a missile, fetch the flock nicely 'to hand' and sit by your side eager for the next command, determined to please.

'Git away bye,' you'll say on Tuesday, and off he'll go like a missile, – back home, leaving you screaming and pleading, threatening, foaming at the mouth, wishing you carried a gun.

'Git away bye,' you'll say on Wednesday, – and he'll sit there looking as if you'd given the order in Swahili. Throw your stick at him and he'll probably pick it up and bury it.

However if I give the impression that sheep dogs can be devious, let me make it clear they aren't in the same league as the characters who sell them.

These men are a special breed, part genius, part gypsy, capable of selling their daughters into the white slave trade.

They'll talk lyrically about the animal's parents and brothers, how one of the last litter won at the Royal Show, and how they really don't want to sell this one, but there are two more pups at home almost as good, and not enough work for them all ... 'dinna want t'spoil such a good dog y'understand,' he'll confide.

Maybe not, but he'll ruin you, – no bother.

My father took me to buy a dog once from a crafty old shepherd on the edge of the world west of Tow Law.

He asked to see the dog 'run' of course, and the fella willingly took us onto the hill behind his house.

'Tremendous bitch,' he said; 'do anything y'ask, tremendously well bred she is.' She looked keen enough to go, –

'work for anybody,' said the shepherd, . . . 'tremendously biddable.'

Way up on the hillside a couple o' hundred yards off about fifty yowes were grazing peacefully, oblivious of what lay in store for them.

'Git away bye Moss,' said the shepherd, and off she went like a shot from a gun.

Now those of you who have a collie dog already, or have at least seen that telly programme, will know that it is desirable for the dog to go wide around behind the sheep, and then gently ease them off back towards the shepherd.

Moss obviously considered this a very slow, boring exercise, and instead headed at great speed straight for the middle of the flock which by now had seen the approaching beast and were showing signs of apprehension.

It was pretty obvious what was going to happen, but the shepherd appeared remarkably unconcerned. At the last moment, however, just before the dog reached the sheep, he stepped forward and shouted, 'Split them, Moss!' And she did, – into about fifty groups of one, many of them upside down.

Father didn't buy that dog, but he did purchase another called Dick (who later acquired other names, – but we won't go into that). Dick *could* be quite brilliant, courageous with cattle, not too savage with sheep, – and when in the mood, nowt would get past 'im.

The trouble was the mood left him occasionally, and when it did he generally left as well.

This invariably happened at the far end of the farm when I was about to bring a bunch of ewes and lambs or some in-calf heifers back home to dose or dip, or whatever. Just when he was needed most, Dick would sneak off.

No amount of promising or persuasion would stop him; he'd either give his slanty-eyed farewell look and leave, or he'd be gone before I even noticed. He'd come back of course, often very late at night, looking decidedly weary.

A neighbouring shepherd and dog breeder heard about this problem and recommended a pocketful of cheese as the certain cure.

Dogs

'Always carry a bit o'cheese with y',' he said. 'Doesn't have t'be anythin' fancy, a chunk of Co-op yellow will do nicely, – that dog'll never leave your side, as long as y' carry a bit o'cheese.'

For weeks I wandered about reeking of cheese, – with my pockets all torn where Dick had tried to get at the Co-op yellow. It couldn't last. Dick soon learned to hang about (but threatening to leave all the time), until as a desperate bribe to stay, he would be offered the cheese. He'd gulp it down in one swallow, *then* he'd leave, smiling. He seemed to know when there was none left.

Sweep was the best dog I ever had, brave and never 'huffy' even when I threw things at him.

He could've been a champion trial dog I think, but he would've needed a different master if we had ever been invited to perform on 'One Man and His Dog'. My detailed instructions to Sweep, or any other collie, have always been punctuated by loud and desperate swear words, and, depending on the intelligence of the dog, they've generally been fully understood. However with umpteen million viewers the BBC would have been obliged to censor most of my effort, or put it on after midnight when old ladies and impressionable children are away to bed.

Nevertheless Sweep was a hard-working dog, and almost indestructible. I remember we were once walking some cattle to Alnwick Mart (yes it was a long time ago), – a four-mile journey full of hazards that included two narrow bridges, the A1, irate housewives in Duke Street who didn't appreciate heifers at the bottom of their gardens and Tommy Ord's school bus which travelled the same route as us at the same time, about the same speed, permanently enveloped in a cloud of black smoke.

As we approached one of the bridges I noticed the fence was broken down at the far end. If the cattle went through they'd be off into the wood and we'd never get to the mart, – so I ordered the brave Sweep to go past and guard the hole. Obeying instantly he leapt over the parapet of the bridge, which he presumably thought was a small wall, – and plummeted thirty feet to the rocky river bed below.

He survived with four lacerated feet, and I had to carry him the rest of the way to Alnwick, whimpering softly (Sweep that is, not me).

The vet was bewildered. 'What happened?' he asked.

'The dog jumped over the bridge,' I said.

'What on earth did he do that for?'

'Well I suppose because I told him to . . .' I said.

The vet gave me a very funny look. 'You're not fit to have a dog,' he said.

Meanwhile the heifers were nibbling herbaceous borders in Duke Street, and by the time I got back to them the final fuchsia had gone.

Sweep was obviously in a class of his own, a rare creature, happy to follow me about all day, just out of throwing range. His life was complete if I patted him on the head and muttered anything remotely complimentary. He had a disarming smile.

After a succession of brainless, cardiac-inducing hounds who simply ate, slept and seduced, and were never available in a crisis, – I came to the conclusion that no dog at all was better than a moderate one.

A final indication of the dangers to your health and sanity that can ensue if you persist with collie dogs and are then perhaps tempted into the Show arena is given by our friend the agricultural correspondent of the *Clartiehole and District Gazette* in the following report of a recent sheep-dog trial at a local show.

There were no television cameras there, he writes, just farmers and shepherds in their best suits carrying fancy sticks, – and devoted collie dogs. The organising committee had found five mad fit young sheep and they were standing up on the hillside waiting to be 'shepherded'. The object of the exercise, as usual, was to fetch these sheep down the hill, through a couple of gates, into the main ring, and eventually put all five of them into a little pen, – specially designed to hold four.

Willie Anderson was the first fella to have a go. There he

stood quietly confident at the starting post, saying 'git away bye' to his dog Spot.

And Spot did just that, he got away bye right enough. He went like something possessed, away up the hill, straight past the sheep (who watched him with considerable interest as he flashed by), past the Land Rovers and horse-boxes parked up there, over a stone wall, across a ploughed field and, still going like the wind, through a thorn hedge on the horizon, – and vanished.

He probably slowed down when he got to the river Tweed, but to the best of my knowledge he's never been seen since.

You could tell Willie was 'disappointed'. He screamed and pleaded and prayed for Spot to 'sit down' and 'cum bye' until, sobbing pitifully, they took him away to the St John Ambulance tent for treatment.

It was Arthur Thompson's turn next, and they had to get *him* out of the beer tent, and guide him to the starting post.

Nevertheless Arthur and his dog began fairly well. Between them they got the sheep down the hill and through the gates pretty quick 'n' easy. Perhaps it was a bit *too* quick 'n' easy, – and sure enough, just when things seemed to be going really well, the sheep saw a little gap, pricked their lugs, and bolted off into the car park.

Arthur was foamin', the language was terrible, he even threw his stick at the dog, but he missed, and it went banging into the front door of a big blue Volvo belonging to one of the judges.

But Arthur was past caring, – he went running after the sheep himself, rantin' and ravin', and a couple of minutes later he came staggering back carrying one of the poor bewildered sheep. Still swearing, he hurled it into the little pen, gave it a vicious kick up the backside, – and then with his sore foot hobbled away back to the beer tent muttering dire threats to his dog.

His dog hid under one of the cars and said nothing.

Sep and Sweep very nearly made it. There was no shouting or swearing, just the occasional whistle and a bit of encouragement, – and Sweep brought the sheep gently right down to the very edge of the pen. There he was, eyes bright, nose to the ground, easing them in, – Sep ready to swing the gate shut and take the applause.

It was at this moment that a nymphomaniac border terrier from North Shields came trotting through the legs of those who were watching, and started to 'chat up' Sweep.

Well, the auld collie didn't have a chance, did he? Sweep probably figured this was far too good an opportunity to miss, – so the two of them left together smiling, with that meaningful look in their eyes.

The sheep left as well of course, there was nothing to keep them; they went away back up the hill, – and Sep wandered off slowly to join Arthur in the beer tent. He was trying desperately to look as if it didn't really matter.

'Where's your dog?' asked Arthur from behind another pint.

'I think the randy bugger's away on his honeymoon,' said Sep, – 'and if he's got any sense he'll not come home for a day or two either!'

As Charles Kingsley wrote long ago . . .

When all the world is young lad,
and all the trees are green;
And every goose a swan lad,
And every lass a queen;
Then hey for boot and horse lad,
And round the world away;
Young blood must have its course lad,
And every dog his day.

With a Little Help
From Your Friends . . .

You can beg steal or borrow
and pay back tomorrow
a nod is as good as a wink
the banker's your friend
and eager to lend
provided your job's index-linked –

But a peasant of course
is a quite different horse
a species that's almost extinct
he goes down on his knees
and politely says please
'cos he tends to be overdraft-linked

Everybody needs some help now and then, and peasants are no exception. In an industry that has 'progressed' like a bat out of hell over the past fifty years, with new machines, new techniques, new sciences and new production records, – you're going to need a bit of support, at least in the early stages.

This part of the book then is devoted to some of the people whom you're bound to 'trip over' in business, and attempts to advise the beginner in his relationships with them.

Bank Manager
First, and more important than all others is your bank manager. Without this charming, helpful, handsome, benevolent,

witty, enlightened genius, – you ain't gonna make it, so be nice to him.

If he fancies living in your cupboard, – fair enough. If he suggests a round of golf, by all means, – but let him beat you by at least 5 and 4. Never interrupt him when he's talking, especially if it's rubbish, and always fall off your chair when he tells a joke.

Of course he may not be too familiar with the subtle art of picking wild oats, or delivering a crazy gimmer of twins coming backwards on a wet night in March, – but he will be able to count up to ten without using his fingers, and is unlikely to be over-impressed if you present your cash-flow forecast scratched on the back of a fag packet with a 3½ inch nail.

Most peasants compare a visit to the bank manager with a trip to the dentist, or afternoon tea with the Ayatollah Khomeini, but sadly there is no way you can avoid (at least) the periodic inquisition on your overdraft, – and when he calls, you gotta go.

In order to give the fledgling peasant some idea of what this traumatic event entails, I have included here an episode from the experiences of an older 'seasoned' campaigner who is no longer entirely over-awed by the occasion (in fact he might even be a trifle under-awed).

As usual the phone rang just as Sep was about to sit down for his dinner.

'Yes?' he barked into the receiver, – he always answered it like that, short and sharp. It frightened the life out of gossiping women and 'crawling' reps. In earlier days Gladys's mother would be so shaken whenever Sep answered, she would often apologise for dialling the wrong number and promptly hang up.

This time however it was different.

'Oh good morning,' he said, 'how are you? Yes thanks, fine, yes she's very well . . . uh uh not bad, canny . . . what's that? Oh right enough, – a drop of rain would do no harm at all. . . .'

Gladys, listening from the kitchen, was quite bewildered.

Who on earth could it be? . . . him being so polite and speaking in proper English, – must be somebody very special. A picture of the Queen Mother flashed through her mind.

'What d'y say?' he went on . . . 'oh yes certainly, any time y'like, uh uh, aye well next time I'm in then, I'll give y'a ring . . . right then cheerio, ta ta. . . .'

She heard the receiver go back on the cradle, and Sep came back along the passage, sat down, and attacked his cool mince.

'He's a smooth auld bugger,' he grunted.

'Who?' said Gladys eagerly.

'That Jimmy Duckworth at the bank, that was him on the phone, – only rings up when you're stretched a bit, never when you're flush. . . . Wonders if we might have a little chat, he says, nothin' serious he says (like a surgeon who's gonna take your leg off), – just thought it was about time we discussed your requirements for the year . . . no hurry, he says, next time you're in town will do nicely, he says.'

For the next three months Sep was seldom in town, and if he was, he generally stayed in the car with his collar turned up like a gangster, while Gladys did the shopping.

A couple of times he *was* obliged to go into the bank, but he ensured he was heavily disguised, looked neither left nor right, spoke to no one, and departed very quickly.

The subtle disguise for the first visit was to get washed and shaved, and put his suit on. Nobody recognised him at all; some customers giggled a bit at the suit with its trousers at half-mast and the jacket only meeting at the top button, but no one said anything.

The second time he wore an old black duffle coat that reached almost to the floor, with the hood up and Gladys's reading glasses. He resembled an ageing nun. The glasses made it difficult for him to see at all, and he almost got into trouble as he groped his way along a queue of old ladies waiting for their travellers' cheques.

Mr Duckworth 'caught' him on the third visit. He had

the suit on again, but had forgotten to change his wellies, and perhaps the familiar aroma had wafted into the manager's office.

'Ah Sep, how good of you to call,' said the dreaded voice, – 'have you a few minutes? Good, splendid, just come in, you're very lucky, I haven't any appointments for the rest of the afternoon.'

Sep, who'd had a few 'nips' at the Swan after the mart, didn't really consider himself all *that* lucky, but followed like a schoolboy summoned to the headmaster's study.

There was one of those incomprehensible farmers' balance sheets lying on the desk ready to be filled in, together with Sep's personal file.

'Take a seat, sit down,' said Mr Duckworth, – 'not too early for a small sherry, eh?'

'Whisky,' said Sep, – it was likely to be a rough session, so he might as well get what he could while the going was fairly good.

The suspicion of impending doom was confirmed when Duckworth found he couldn't open the drinks cabinet . . . 'lost the key,' he smiled, 'sometimes rattles open though, sometimes it doesn't, . . . will tea do?'

Sep had his 'lambs foot' knife out before the man could ring for his secretary; a little educated fiddle at the lock and the door was open. It was all over and Sep back in his chair, knife folded away, drink in hand, before Duckworth could blink.

Sep downed the first one offered, and got a refill.

'Well then,' said Duckworth still full of charm, pencil poised, – 'the same acreage is it?' Sep nodded, '. . . and sheep, – I see this time last year you had about two hundred ewes . . . more or less the same is it?'

'More or less,' said Sep as coolly as he could; he'd finished the second glass, and was feeling much better.

'Well we'll say two hundred then, – alright?'

'Aye well, maybe hardly as many as that,' – he wanted to giggle, '. . . er, say about forty-three.'

'Forty-three!' spluttered Duckworth.

'Well t'be honest a few o'*them* aren't too bright,' said Sep, – 'a lot of staggers about y'know . . .'

'But what on earth have you done with the rest of them?' Duckworth was eating his pencil.

'Well,' said Sep, trying to sound philosophical, – 'it's been a hard winter y'know, and then some of them got into the meal store one night and . . .!'

'What happened to them?' asked Duckworth, and immediately wished he hadn't.

'They died!' said Sep, looking at the man as if he must be a congenital idiot to ask such a question, – 'they ate a belly-full of barley, blew up, and died!'

'How about the cattle?' Duckworth was apprehensive now, – 'last time you had, er, let me see . . . thirty weaned calves, forty-five stores and twenty ready to sell fat . . . don't tell me they got into the meal store as well. . . .'

'Oh no,' said Sep, 'well not many anyway, – but we haven't any fat ones, 'cos they've all had a touch of pneumonia y'see . . . didn't do them any good.'

Duckworth was wheezing regularly himself by now, and when Sep helped himself to a fourth glass of Glenfiddich, he quickly screwed the top back on the bottle and put it away in a drawer.

Sep felt much more at ease, – a drink or two in the middle of the day always made him feel relaxed and dozy, – 'I've got a bit of corn to shell, I mean sell, – could be fifty tons in the shed.' He decided not to mention the mouldy smell and the big green patch under the hole in the roof.

'And we've got some hay left over,' he said cheerfully, 'in fact we've got a right big heap of it.' No need to tell the man all the strings were rotten and nobody could pick it up . . . 'and straw's a hellova price,' he added; 'y'can get whatever y'ask for straw.'

Duckworth (clutching at straws), brightened slightly. 'You have some straw to sell?' he asked.

'No,' said Sep, 'nobody has any straw, that's why it's such a hellova price!' He was finding it harder not to giggle.

Duckworth moved desperately to the statement, 'I see

you're overdrawn well past your limit.' He sounded like a second-hand car dealer inspecting a trade-in without an MoT.

'No use having a limit if you never get to it,' said Sep. He was leaning well over the desk now, and could see several Duckworths, but felt supremely confident he could outwit all of them.

'But you're *past* your limit,' chorused all the Duckworths.

'There y' are then,' said Sep proudly, 'just shows what y' can do if you try. . . .'

'I don't think you understand,' the manager was disappointed at the way the interview was going; '. . . we can't possibly lend you any more money until this overdraft of yours is substantially reduced, and what's more . . .'

'Wait a minute,' interrupted Sep, 'wait a minute.' He pointed his finger at the middle Duckworth. 'What would happen if nobody ever borrowed any money from you lot, eh? What would happen then, eh?'

'That's not the point,' said Mr Duckworth.

Sep moved his finger, 'I'll tell you what would happen Jimmy m' old mate, – your bloody bank would be shooper-fluous that's what; y'd go bust, broke, – isn't that right now?'

'Well perhaps, but . . .'

'Never mind perhaps matey, – your bank needs blokes like me, – no good all them rich buggers just pourin' money into here, and you sittin' on it like an auld clocker, is there?'

Mr Duckworth leaned over, brought out the whisky again and filled his own glass with a shaky hand.

'But you must realise,' he said as calmly as he could, 'we can't let all our customers borrow just what they like and never pay us back.'

'What about Brazil 'n' Mexico?' said Sep.

'Brazil!' exclaimed Mr Duckworth, his eyebrows moving up to where his hair used to be, '. . . Mexico! – what on earth has Mexico got to do with *your* overdraft?' A terrifying thought struck him, – 'you haven't bought a coffee plantation without telling me have you?' he asked.

'Of course not,' said Sep, – 'but y'let *them* get away wi' millions, and all I want is a few quid till I sell some barley!'

Mr Duckworth looked at his watch. He was getting one of his headaches. He longed for the peace and quiet of his neat home on the neat estate, and the comfort of his loving wife. He began to think of early retirement, his pension, pruning roses and taking the dog for a walk. . . .'

'How much do you need?' he asked wearily.

Accountant

It's all too easy to be impressed by your accountant. If you're a simple peasant with a limited education, there is a natural tendency to over-estimate someone who appears to understand mathematics. Although these characters may well be able to 'add up' and 'take away' quicker than the average horse, they often haven't a clue about the complex world of agriculture, – and, worse still, the Inland Revenue confuses some of them as well.

So your choice of 'bookkeeper' is important.

It's no good just wandering into the offices of Messrs Grumble, Greanfly and Gormless and saying, 'do y' fancy doin' m' books mister?' Old Bernie Greanfly will be delighted to make your acquaintance, might even offer you cocoa and a digestive, – and before you can mutter 'P.45' you'll be one of his regiment of tame clients, all doing what they're told, signing everything put in front of them, their accounts a decade out of date, and paying more tax than ICI.

Beware too of the charming young man with the friendly smile and an autographed photo of Wedgie Benn on the wall, who operates from a dusty office with a one-watt light bulb, above the local massage parlour. He'll be the agent for the Netherwitten Building Society, treasurer of the cricket club, and probably a very good husband and father. He could also be a devout left-wing socialist plotting a coup d'état in which the land owners are all annihilated.

He's the sort who is constantly at war with the tax inspector, and that's disastrous.

What you want is some sneaky little bespectacled scoundrel, as devious and crafty as a Philadelphia lawyer, half computer, half Robot. Someone who enjoys cooking up figures that no one but he can comprehend, explanations that make no sense to anyone else, whose sole object in life is to ensure you hang on to whatever you make, whose opinion of the collector is summed up in a couple of dirty words, but can 'smarm' his way through any problem.

This nasty, unnattractive accountant will cost you a bob or two, but he's worth looking for, – even if you have to wait until he gets out of Pentonville.

Vets

There will be occasions in your dealings with dumb animals, when loving care and dedicated husbandry are not enough. They get sick like you and me, but of course they find it more difficult to tell us where it hurts.

For instance you may have this pathetic pot-bellied calf that won't eat and falls down every time it coughs. You've given him every vaccine and antibiotic left over from earlier disasters (even if the expiry dates were historical), searched among the dust on top of the kitchen cupboard for patent worm powders and calf elixirs, poured half a gallon of Epsom salts down his throat, and given him a damn good hiding with a fork shank, – all to no avail.

The vet, with all his years of training and experience, his vast fund of scientific knowledge, his collection of James Herriot paperbacks and a car boot full of penicillin is your only hope, your last resort.

'What seems to be the trouble?' he asks confidently.

'Well vet, it's this 'ere calf,' you say as you open the door of the 'loose-box' to reveal the hopeless case.

He examines it carefully, thermometer, stethoscope, pokes here, prods there, peers into eyes and ears and mouth, administers a few intravenous injections, a dozen bright red pills, a foul-smelling drench, and steps back. The diagnosis is swift and sure, reinforced by those years of training and experience, – it's all assessed in a moment, he's seen it all before.

'Well,' you ask hopefully.

'It's a knacker-job,' he says without opening his mouth, – and you get a bill for thirty quid.

To be fair though, sick cattle can often be cured, and sometimes respond to the magic of medicine.

With sheep of course it's entirely different, here you can save yourself a hatful of money by not bothering your hard-pressed overworked vet at all. The patient will inevitably die, probably as he drives into the yard, – so you'll still get a bill.

However there are exceptions to every rule, – and it might be reassuring to the apprentice shepherd to include here a little story which first appeared in a publication called *A Load of Rural Rubbish* way back in 1972.

According to the writer of that 'epic', it appears there was once a kind-hearted friendly peasant, who lived with his devoted wife and three lovable children, in a delightful old farm nestling by a little stream, that flowed gently to the big blue sea far away.

Each morning he would go off into the fields to work, whistling a happy tune, and in the evening his devoted wife would have his supper ready on the kitchen table. Then he would sit by the log fire and tell stories to his three lovable children, until it was time to climb into bed. (You may have realised already that this is a fairy story.)

Anyway, one day while tending his flock in the meadow, he noticed that his favourite mule ewe was looking very unhappy. She lay under a tree neither grazing nor sleeping, and hung her head as if the problems of the world were resting on her shoulders. (Well, at least that's a familiar picture.)

So like all good shepherds he carried the poor animal home, and putting her in a warm bed of clean straw, he gave her a pint of Doctor Quicklift's Patent Sheep Reviver, patted her on the head and went happily to his sleep, confident she'd be well again in the morning. (You can see he wasn't very bright, can't you?)

Next day he woke early, and kissing his devoted wife and

three lovable children he went whistling off to work again. (No, he's not for real.)

On this morning he went straight to the old byre where his favourite ewe lay poorly, – alas she was no better (surprise, surprise).

Undismayed he went again to his old medicine cupboard and brought out Professor Queerthings Sickness Powers, and mixing them carefully with a gallon of warm brown ale, he quickly persuaded the ewe to drink it down.

Still she failed to rally, and her eyes remained closed. 'There's only one thing left to do,' said the peasant, – 'I'll have to get the vet.'

'It's fluke,' said the vet. 'Yes, fluke, that's what it is alright, no doubt about it; or possibly pulpy kidney, yes it could be pulpy kidney . . . unless of course it's a cobalt deficiency, there's a lot of that about just now . . . or staggers perhaps, – that's what it'll be, staggers. Then again mind you it might be foot and mouth, or even fowl pest, – you can never be too sure with mule ewes y'know. But fear not, we'll soon have her up and about again, good as new.'

The peasant was less confident by now, in fact he was a worried man, and his devoted wife and lovable children were sobbing pitifully at the byre door, – what would happen if the old ewe stopped, never to go again? (Try to imagine plaintive violin music at this point.)

However, the vet was undismayed, and he gave the sheep fourteen injections, a gallon of drench, thirty-eight bright yellow pills, covered her feet with Stockholm tar, wrapped a hot bran poultice round her head, and drove off in his big car singing 'It's the rich what get the pleasure and the poor what get the blame'.

For days and days the peasant nursed his favourite ewe, never leaving her side for food or sleep. Special prayers were offered by the Archbishop, and the WI choir came to the byre door and sang 'ewe'll never walk alone'.

But after a fortnight even the friendly kind-hearted peasant could stand no more of this, – he 'snapped'. (Who wouldn't?)

He kicked the old ewe right up the alleyway and out of the byre. 'Stuff *you*,' he roared, 'you dozy auld git, – I'm sick of y'!' With that he strode back into the house without taking his wellies off, ate his supper without a word, opened a bottle of whisky, lit a fag, turned the telly over to Sportsnight, and ordered his three wailing kids to bed. (Now that's more like it, isn't it?)

Next morning there in the garden stood his favourite old ewe, eating the lawn, several primulas and all the cabbage plants. She'd had twins.

The vet concealed his surprise very well of course (it's part of their training y'know), and duly claimed all the credit. But *he* knew and the *peasant* knew and the *auld yow* knew, that this was just another of life's little miracles. We all need them now and then.

Auctioneers

Although you may never get to know your local auctioneer particularly well, the chances are that before long he'll know more about you than your own mother. It'll take him about a week to discover how dodgy your bank balance is, or whether you know the difference between a Charolais bullock and a Swaledale Chaser, or if it doesn't matter anyway, 'cos your wife owns half of General Motors.

He is by nature, and profession, a blatherer, and almost everything he says is unintelligible (at least to the beginner). The language of auctioneers is unique, and it's essential that the budding peasant becomes bilingual as soon as possible.

Here are a few useful phrases in auctionese:

'*Grand shifters off high ground*,' means 'I know they look as if they haven't had a decent feed all year, but if you give them a bale of hay they might live.'

'*Stand on, anybody will*,' freely translated means 'any fool who bid for the last lot, has to have a go here. . . .'

'*I wouldn't take y'twice Sir*,' means he's probably had you bidding against yourself for the last ten minutes; and '*we can't go at this price lads*,' often suggests the only person bidding is himself. Enthusiastic expressions such as 'watta pen!' or 'watta bullock!' or whatever, are simply designed to boost the ego of the seller, and draw the buyer's attention away from the lame hogg hobbling about in the middle of the ring, or the uncastrated suckler vainly trying to rape the weighbridge.

If the trade is good (fast), he'll not pause for breath, – the job is easy, peasants and dealers are waving at him from all directions, desperate to catch his eye, and 'get in'. He can take bids from the starlings nesting in the roof some days, and no one would be any the wiser.

'It's on fire,' the buyers will say, – but they'll bid as if this was the very last mart.

If he's struggling in a bad trade (slow), he'll accuse the assembled throng of cowardice, lack of judgement, blindness even. 'There's a bloody fortune left in those beasts,' he'll claim. 'Wake up,' he'll shout, 'these are for nowt, – y'haven't seen them yet!'

It should be pointed out that he may not be the best judge of that, after all he is somewhat biased, – he gets a percentage of whatever you spend. If you go crackers, he's not complaining.

. . . Have You Heard the One About the Commercial Traveller . . .?

One day a farmer (not a million miles from here), was lying under his combine trying to repair a troublesome gearbox, or clutch or something. His tractorman was helping, and the two of them had been hammering and cursing away under the machine all morning, cold and stiff, – when a 'rep' drove into the field.

It was an inopportune moment to sell anything, and if the man had possessed but the brain of a breeze-block, he would've simply gone away at the first sound of a muffled obscenity. But no, he was very young, very enthusiastic, and very thick.

The farmer looked up from under the combine and recognised the bloke. He wouldn't have said anything normally, but he had a bone to pick with him.

'No use you coming here,' he grunted, 'that stuff you sold me last month didn't work properly, – but I'm busy, I'll see you some other time.'

That was the rep's second opportunity to 'pass', – but he dived in.

'What d' y' mean?' he asked, 'that spray always does the job, – are you sure you followed the instructions on the can?'

'We did,' said the farmer, shuffling back towards the gearbox.

'Are you absolutely sure?' persisted the rep, 'because although we try to make it as simple as possible, – we sometimes find that farmers and farm workers are illiterate y'know. . . .'

Now whether this was the man's idea of a joke or not we'll

71

never know, – because he just had time to scramble back into his car and roar backwards out of the gate, before being assassinated by two peasants wielding large spanners.

I knew another farmer however, who although more or less 'normal' in most ways, had a positive fear of commercial travellers. He reckoned he simply hadn't time to listen to their chat, – but it was a bit more than that. He would 'hide' when he saw one approaching, pretend to be very busy changing an oil filter (for the fourth time that week), or roar off on a tractor to nowhere in particular, but over a wet ploughed field, where salesmen are reluctant to go. Or he would just disappear up the back-end of a combine, or sit under a wuffler until the coast was clear. He'd always take a hammer with him just in case he was discovered.

I can sympathise with him a bit. I've got nothing against 'reps' in general. Most of them know when to appear, when to stay clear, when to give you their patter, but there are some, who even in the face of undiluted abuse and rampant sales resistance, still turn up with a sickly smile, thick-skinned and moronic, pouring out their own brand of Party Political Broadcast. These characters are pests, – like leather jackets.

Fortunately they're easily recognised and their behaviour predictable. Their general appearance can be quite impressive. The peasant customer (probably covered in grease and hen muck), can look like a drop-out by comparison.

They often wear a sort of Point-to-Point outfit: cavalry twill trousers with a sharp crease, checked sports jacket and shirt, – and a 'conversational' tie, that looks as if it's something special, but isn't.

They drive clean company Sierras (or maybe Montegos now), the back seat covered with a mass of irrelevant and unreadable literature, on how you should rear your pigs, or spray your winter wheat, – and the boot crammed with samples of their 'unique' product.

This character will drive into the yard when you're dosing deranged sucklers, or clipping sheep, or mending a burst water pipe, – when you're disinclined to blather to Miss United Kingdom let alone a 'clever' salesman.

Even more serious perhaps is the occasion when he comes to the door on a fine afternoon, as you are lazily watching the Test Match or Wimbledon. No good pretending you're not in, or down with the flu, because he's seen you through the window, and in any case the wife has answered the door already. You simply have to get up and face the creep, trying to hide your in-bred guilt (*you* know you shouldn't be sitting in the house at this time of day, and so does *he*, – and it gives him an edge).

'Ah Mr (whatever it is),' he beams, 'didn't really expect to catch you today I'm from Flukonak International and as you know we supply new improved biological foot-rot paste and recent tests in Botswanaland have shown that this unique formula can stop ringworm warble flies and acne what's more it can be used as a winter lubricant for your tractor and a splendid filling for vol-au-vents and sandwich cakes.'

He says this without punctuation and with a permanent smile on his face, which can't be easy, – but they're specially trained.

He produces a notebook from his shining brief case. 'You'll see several of your neighbours are already customers of ours,' he'll say, – and there before your very eyes is a list of blokes caught with their resistance down, who should've known better.

If you're foolish enough to buy anything, he'll be back again, and again and again. If you don't actually buy, but respond in any way to his patter, he'll be there till dark. Never ever be trapped by his flattery . . . 'My word you have the best field of oil seed rape in the county,' – or, 'those are tremendous lambs, the fittest I've seen this year . . .' can lull you into an unrealistic sense of well-being, and you might even begin to like the bloke.

Never indicate success and solvency to a visiting rep, deny any profit.

Ideally I suppose he should find you sitting at the farm

gate wearing a pair of dark glasses with your cap on the ground in front of you, and playing a fiddle, with your faithful collie dog by your side. However, if he does catch you unawares and there's no escape, paint a picture of absolute despair and desolation. This leaves the impression that even if he *did* persuade you to buy something from him, he'd never get paid.

Any conversation forced upon you should be conducted as follows (totally ignoring the rep until he speaks first of course).

'Good afternoon,' he'll chirp, 'how are things with you?'

'Terrible.'

'Oh dear, I'm sorry to hear that.' (He's still smiling though.)

'Aye the bank's not very chuffed either.'

'Well perhaps I can interest you in . . .'

'Not so loud son, – the wife's not too fit t'day. . . .'

'Oh, nothing serious I hope?'

'No, just a touch of anthrax.'

'Well if I just show you a sample of . . .'

'Watch the dog.'

'The dog?'

'Rabies!'

'Good lord, I'll leave you my card then . . . 'bye.'

From this you will gather that most 'normal' peasants dislike salesmen, not only because they intrude uninvited at inconvenient moments, – but because (though reluctant to admit it), we simply couldn't do *their* job, even if paid a king's ransom or a pitman's redundancy. Although sales and advertising are perfectly respectable professions, and sometimes very rewarding, – farmers tend to view that area as 'poncie' and 'parasitic'.

The sentimental townie is a sucker especially when animals are concerned, and we all have to put up with the sickly ads in which pampered pussies eat caviar from the best silver, and cuddly puppies test the wet strength of endless toilet rolls. But for the mercenary farmers the attraction has to be the promise of hard cash.

'Martin Mildew, who farms 5,000 acres in Berkshire uses 68N, – Britain's favourite fertiliser.' 'Since I changed to 68N,' says he, 'my yields have trebled.' And there's a picture of Martin, clean 'n' tidy, grinning from a sea of barley. We know he's a lying toad of course, but we buy the stuff.

Over the page, again in glorious technicolour, we find another rustic 'genius', surrounded by sheep, and up to his armpits in rampant ryegrass. 'After spraying all my fields with Polyglot extra,' he claims, 'there's not a weed on the farm' (and all his family are free of dandruff as well no doubt).

It's the image of success that sells, the ad-man would never be interested in the ordinary genuine peasant. It just wouldn't look right to have some poor destitute bloke standing there, sobbing pitifully, among his broken-down flock, syringe in one hand, spade in the other, saying, 'since I used Flukonak only *half* my sheep have died.'

Official Visitors

All visitors from the *Ministry of Agriculture* and associated bodies should be welcomed in a manner befitting the Pope, the chief constable, or Raquel Welch. In other words be nice to the fella 'cos he may have immense power. A cup of coffee or even a swift 'fry up' could mean the difference between getting the grant on your new concrete silage pit passed, or flung out because it looks suspiciously like a swimming pool. Treat him like a 'rep', and your plans have had it.

I know the *Safety Officer* is a nuisance, – but if he falls into the septic tank for God's sake don't leave him there, even if it does look like a good idea at the time. And if he gets his fingers fast in an unguarded grain auger, – switch it off before he gets really upset; in any case he could jam up the works and burn the motor out. If he falls through the rotten granary floor, don't sue him for damages or claim he was over-weight, – better by far to be very sympathetic, and maybe even promise to visit him in hospital, if there's a wet day.

Sooner or later your name will be drawn from the hat for a *VAT* check-up, and out of a grey sky will come a machiavellian mathematician (who looks about twelve years old), from Customs and Excise. He will inevitably find something wrong with your records. There's no escape, – you've probably been claiming the tax back on your favourite chocolate wholemeal biscuits anyway.

Your best bet is to be charming and pretty stupid. Plead insanity, old age, the sad demise of your collie dog, any-thing, – persuade your wife to serve him tea dressed in suspender belt and a balaclava. Try to ensure he leaves feeling sorry for this poor old deranged git, driven out of his tiny mind by bad luck and an over-demanding woman, and you might get off with a caution, if you pay up immediately in pound notes.

Policemen will occasionally call, perhaps because somebody's pinched your baler, or they suspect you of pinching somebody else's, or you haven't renewed the twelve-bore licence, or you accidentally set fire to a patrol car while burning straw last week, or your sheep are grazing on the M1, or because they just fancy a bag of taties, half a dozen eggs and a cup of coffee. Or maybe (perish the thought), you were observed proceeding in a mart direction with nine fat hoggs in the back of the pickup and one in the front (sir). If the one in the front wasn't wearing a seat belt, you could be in serious trouble.

Plead guilty and throw yourself on the mercy of the magistrates. After all the chairman borrows your muck spreader every year doesn't he? – and Lady Daphne always gets a ton of oats for her gee-gees, and the Colonel still owes you for ten bales of hay.

Case dismissed again.

Living on a farm generally means you will have two or three different *postmen* who will travel your route alternate (or every third) weeks. Their delivery times will vary, and will depend solely on how many cups of tea they drink on the way, and how much gossip they are subjected to (or contribute to). More often than not they will all be cheerful, cheeky and extremely helpful. They do not behave like government employees at all.

Unfortunately they bring a daily assortment of rubbish.

About half of this will be bills which should be quickly dropped into the bottom left-hand drawer of the desk to 'ferment' until some dark, wet, windy night when there's nowt on the telly. Almost all the rest will be made up of advertising circulars, special offers and the like, urging you to buy anything from fertiliser to flowers, steel gates, gas cookers, cultivators and carpets. This must obviously cost somebody a large fortune, especially as it's often on technicolour heavy high-class paper, – which luckily burns quite well.

In the spring you'll receive dire warnings of massive and imminent worm infestations, and only the immediate use of 'Phenobiodrenchokil' (or whatever) can save your flock from instant annihilation.

Your winter corn's going yellow? Fear not, top dress it with a hundred units of this, spray it with twenty gallons of that, – if you haven't heard of it, don't worry, there'll be another leaflet in the post tomorrow.

You will soon learn when sorting through the pile of correspondence just what's worth opening and what isn't. A mart cheque or a subsidy payment shines out (you can almost hear it bleeping). In any case you'll certainly be waiting for it, and it's clawed open feverishly, like a junkie after his 'fix'.

Bills and receipts come in dull characterless brown envelopes.

Anything with ordinary (not typed) writing on, and in a coloured (white or blue) envelope is probably from a relation who lives too far away to afford a phone call, or from that young lady you met at Smithfield last December.

As for any outward flow of mail (which will invariably include a cheque), this obviously should be kept to an absolute minimum, – you can't really afford to pay your bills, and then buy a stamp as well. Better by far to deliver the payments to local tradesmen, and inform others that if they want to be paid this month, to come and get it, – arrange this for a day when you're out.

Basically there are only two *wrong* ways to pay a bill, – not at all, and too soon.

Talking of paying large regular bills, brings us inevitably to your local *Water Authority*. This arthritic elephantine body will probably increase your water charges every alternate month, – and if there was a Nobel prize for inefficiency and waste, – they'd win easy.

Too harsh you think? Unfair? . . . ballcocks!

Here is an organisation which sells and distributes only

one basic commodity, – and they acquire it for *nowt*. They don't have to mine it, or chop it down, or sow it one year and harvest it the next, or even manufacture it from raw materials imported cheaply from Taiwan. It falls out of a dark sky, at very regular intervals!

Alright so they *do* collect the stuff, – but after that it flows through alkethene pipes almost certainly 'moled' in by the peasant, through a meter paid for again and again on a rental basis, into troughs, loos and baths, all plumbed in by you, or me, or a tame plumber.

If anything leaks *you* will be responsible for any repairs, *and* pay for the escaped water as well.

They've got it all ways, they can't possibly lose, – can they? Well it appears they can, if they try really hard, – and they certainly do that.

The way to create a massive cock-up like the Water Authority, is first to build an enormous administrative headquarters covering several acres and reaching up to the nearest rain cloud. Then employ twice as many people as you need, put most of them into little vans, and tell them to meander round the countryside looking for meters and mushrooms.

After that it's apparently desirable to concoct an accounting system that defies understanding, and install a computer that can be blamed without answering back.

It's not even imperative that the sums add up, just stick on a bit more 'environmental charge' or a 'sewage charge' or whatever, – the peasant will pay because he has no choice.

Not to be outdone by these masters of 'fluid' arithmetic, the *Electricity Board* and the *Gas Board* and *British Telecom* will all compete for a large slice of your overdraft. (I would advise any reader with teenage children, especially daughters, to install a coin-operated telephone kiosk next to the fridge.)

Of course the problem with all these public bodies is that they have no competition, – they are not governed by the normal rules of economic survival. They are not responsible to shareholders or (it seems), a bank manager. I don't know who first thought up nationalisation (some hairy left-wing economist I expect, or was it Karl Marx?), – but we should certainly build a statue to his memory, paint it bright red, then drop it down a bottomless pit. It would be a meaningful and symbolic exercise.

Neighbours and Landlords

> *Met him almost every morning*
> *just to grumble for a while*
> *swop a few disasters*
> *in the usual farming style*
> *share odd bits of gossip*
> *leaning on the gate*
> *comparing notes and wisdoms*
> *and expensive old mistakes, —*
> *the barley's lookin' useful*
> *turnips need some rain*
> *lambs a mod'rate trade t'day*
> *that heifer's through again*
> *could use an extra trailer*
> *want a hand to lead that hay*
> *can y'eat a bag of taties*
> *and we'll mend that fence t'day*
> *there was never any bother*
> *give 'n' take for evermore*
> *a farmer needs a bit o'luck*
> *and a canny bloke next door . . .*

It's obviously very important to get on well with those who farm around you. It's no use declaring unilateral independence or patrolling your boundary fences with killer whippets.

Fortunately I have always had perfect neighbours. They never borrow any machinery (largely because it's not *worth* borrowing), and seldom does their livestock stray onto this side of the fence (the fact that there's seldom any grass here helps to keep them at home). On the other hand, although our own emaciated animals have constantly and desperately tried to get at the greener stuff over the hedge, they come up against superb fencing, and are generally too weak to jump over or too stiff to creep under.

I once knew a bloke who had a wayward old ewe who regularly crept through his neighbour's hedge. No matter how many rails or old bits of pig netting he stuffed into the holes, this creature still managed to create another, and squeeze through. She was what's known as a 'raker'.

Eventually in desperation he sat in wait for her, and as the animal wriggled half-way through the fence, he shot her, – and left her there to block the hole. Although no doubt quite satisfying, this is an extreme measure and not seriously recommended, – it could easily become addictive. Better by far to sell the thing.

Back to neighbours. It's helpful to have a successful and progressive farmer next door, because he'll always be trying new techniques and systems, – and you can quietly watch as some of them work and some don't.

Strange though it may seem, it's almost as helpful to have a pea-brained nincompoop as a neighbour as well, – it can be very good for the morale. When you've had a bad week, – cow dead, sold all your barley just as the price goes up a fiver, finished spraying some expensive chemical ten minutes before a thunderstorm, that sort of thing, it's reassuring to see this bloke up the road stuttering steadily from disaster to disaster as usual. I know it shouldn't, but it does make y'feel a bit better.

However beware the 'clever' neighbour who lies in wait behind the hedge as you're out for a quiet evening stroll (probably talking to yourself), – he can catch you off guard, and make you feel silly.

'Now then,' he says from behind a thorn bush, '. . . grand night.'

'Oh, – hallo Charlie, I didn't see you there. Yes, smash-in' night.'

'Just havin' a look at the stock are y'?'

'Er, yes, that's right.'

'Suppose y' know you've got a dead yow, d'y'. . . ?'

'Have I? Oh, well actually I thought there was one missing yesterday. . . .'

'Been lyin' there a fortnight, y'wouldn't find it though, the thistles are a hellova height in that field.' He's in full flight now, he's got you where he wants you, '. . . see your corn's gone flat,' he says (with just the suspicion of a smile).

' 'Tis a bit I suppose,' you bleat; 'of course the rain . . .'

'Ours is standin' nicely, y' maybe put too much fertiliser on . . . doesn't pay y' know. . . .'

'Well perhaps, but . . .'

'How d'y' like them bullocks y' bought on Friday then . . .?'

'Well . . .'

'Too much money I thought, – y' would've got them twenty quid cheaper the week before. . . .'

'Really. . . .'

'Oh yes, they were for nothin' that day, – I got thirty-three for m'self, – monsters they are, twice the size of yours, easily.'

All this time you'll be trying desperately to think of something you've got that's better than his, or some blunder of his that might even the score. But it's no use, he's too quick, – he doesn't give you time for that. 'Gotta go,' he says, 'canna blather here all night, got fifty sheep t'clip before supper.' And off he strides whistling and leaving you feeling totally inadequate.

Of course there's nothing the farming fraternity enjoys more than a neighbourhood whizz-kid who comes unstuck.

Once upon a time, when I was a callow youth and too clever by half, I ignored all the logical local common-sense advice, and bought a batch of very special ewe hoggs from the 'deep south'.

They were a new breed, a genetic cocktail of two or three different varieties, designed to combine the better qualities of all into a long-living, prolific-breeding, magic-milking, super sheep.

They didn't have a name like Cheviot or Swaledale or Mule, – they had a number, – something like MX6 or TC3 I think. It sounds more like a nuclear missile now, and looking back that was fairly appropriate, because the creatures certainly travelled at a hell of a speed. They didn't actually blow up on landing, but there were times when I wished they would.

They were demented.

Go to feed them, and they fled into a heap five deep in the far corner of the field, or indeed another field altogether.

Mating them with my randy Suffolk tup was a problem, as well, – he couldn't catch them. He ran around for weeks, willing and eager with his lip lecherously curled until he was exhausted.

I suppose he must have 'chatted up' a few of them, because we did eventually have a lambing of sorts.

The main flock of old fashioned eight-crop mules performed in the normal way, but the 'missiles', who admittedly hadn't participated in this miracle of nature before, were completely bewildered.

For a start when the 'confinement' began there was none of the usual restless maternal behaviour, – such as wandering off to a private corner somewhere, scratching at the ground, lying down and getting up again. Oh no, apparently convinced that some fiend had tied a stick of gelignite under their tail, they careered about the countryside, constantly looking back for the imminent explosion.

The birth itself was even more traumatic. The would-be mother, by now very distressed, had obviously decided that the best way to rid herself of this inconvenience was to wait for darkness (and a blizzard if possible), drop her offspring into a pool of sleet, and run away. However the lamb, having taken a tentative peep out into this bleak world and carefully considered the prospects of life in the 'tender' care of a crazy mother, invariably decided to stay where he was and hang himself.

Shepherds will know that for economic reasons alone you cannot allow this to happen; you have to catch the ewe and assist with elementary midwifery. With these animals it wasn't easy, – it required the talents of an 'All Black' wing forward.

The whole exercise was a disaster, and in farming circles it is impossible to hide disasters.

'Had a good lambin'?' asks this bloke at the mart.

'Well canny y'know, – not bad.'

'Aye, heard y' had some bother wi' them South Country hoggs y'bought.' He was smiling already.

'Well they *were* a bit wild, took some handling.'

'We heard y' couldn't catch them.' He was giggling now.

'Yes, they were a bit "flighty",' I said.

'They tell me only half of them lambed.' There were tears rolling down his face, and he was nudging the fella standing next to him, who was laughing quite openly; 'y' should've stuck with the mules, son.'

'You're probably right,' I said weakly.

'Oh, it's right enough.' He was wiping his eyes and pulling himself together. 'We had a grand lambin'; those old yowes just lamb themselves y' know, – never any bother.'

I hated that man for weeks, – until I realised that 'all hell' would inevitably catch up with him sooner or later, and serve 'im right.

Older and a wee bit wiser now, I realise that all peasants *need* the occasional disaster (somebody else's of course), to keep them more or less sane. It's a relief to hear about a 'cock-up' down the road, – nothing too serious you understand, and certainly nothing personal. It's just a sort of safety-valve. For instance everybody has the odd dead yow, – but it's somehow reassuring to see that Willie too has a couple lying in his front field (with a crow in attendance). You'll say nowt of course (if you've any sense), pretend you didn't notice, – because to mention it tempts the angry gods, and chances are you'll have another dead'n yourself in the morning.

I remember one harvest time years ago anxiously waiting for the contractor's combine to arrive. It would be windy I expect, the barley heads would be blowing off in their thousands, and I would be on the brink of a cardiac convinced I'd be ruined within the hour. I don't suppose I'd be speaking to anybody, – swearing perhaps, and kicking the kids at regular intervals. Just a normal harvest day.

Eventually I couldn't hang about any longer, and set off in the car to 'find' the combine. I knew where he was, and he should have been finished there ages ago.

Sure enough when I saw him he was into the 'butts', only about an acre to go, so I walked across, much calmer now, and climbed aboard.

I was riding on the step blathering away to the driver, when into the field came the bloke who was 'leading off'. He left his tractor and trailer parked by the gate, and jumped up onto the combine as well. The three of us were discussing record yields, the weather, and the state of the nation, when we suddenly noticed that the tractor and trailer were moving down the hillside, – he'd obviously left the brake off.

We stopped to watch, but the tractor didn't. It gathered speed and bounced its way towards the fence.

'It's gonna hit that tree,' I said, 'it'll be a write-off.' I was quite excited at the prospect.

'No it won't,' said the combine driver very calmly, 'it's going all the way to the road.'

'Never,' said the tractorman, 'it'll cowp before it gets that far.'

Well it missed the tree, smashed through the fence, took off from the sod cast, and landed on the other side of the road no more than three feet in front of my parked car.

Then it cowped, – and wrecked the car.

The message is simple: you can't really avoid the occasional disaster, – but if the man next door has one, for God's sake don't laugh, at least not till he's out of sight.

Which brings us to the *Landlord*. No need to tell you this gentleman calls for special treatment.

Even if he isn't actually a real live Duke, it'll do no harm to address him as 'your grace' or at least 'yer 'onour'.

With a bit of luck he won't bother you too often so long as you pay the rent and resist any temptation to turn the buildings into a rehabilitation centre for destitute chorus girls.

When he does appear it's of paramount importance that he gets the right impression.

Nothing is more likely to upset 'his grace' than a tenant who is obviously better off than himself, – he'll have your rent increased before you can utter arbitration. Here then are a few simple suggestions for a landlord's visit.

First conceal your new car under any available straw stack, then take your tractor up to the local garage, and having picked out the most decrepit beat-up van from the pile of scrap at the back, tow it down to your front door for the day. Next remove whatever respectable machinery you may have into the nearest wood, and go round all the dyke-backs and retrieve the old harrows and rakes, and park them neatly in the implement shed. If you can borrow a few old moulting rhode-island reds to sit on this rusty gear as well, so much the better, – it adds to the picture of rustic hardship.

It might also help if you can arrange for your dear devoted wife to take in some washing that day (no automatic machine of course, – only a poss tub and an old mangle). Hide the kids' wellies so that they can be observed chopping kindlin' in their bare feet, dressed only in very short holey vests, cold and miserable.

Needless to say you must remove the telly, the video, and the old Leonardo da Vinci masterpiece from over the fireplace, and indeed anything that might suggest you're more or less solvent. By all means be courteous, offer the man some refreshment, but restrict this to a small glass of home-made turnip wine, or a cup of luke-warm tea served in a cracked Mickey Mouse mug. After all this he'll still put your rent up of course, – but if he's got any soul at all, it should be a modest rise in line with your pathetic lifestyle and apparent lack of ambition.

'The agent'

> Wellies green
> good tweed suit
> Cirencester tie
> clean checked shirt
> flat brown cap
> worn just above the eye, –
> landlord's voice
> tenant's ear
> let and arbitrate
> kitchen sink
> hemmel roof
> rural real estate, –
> CLA
> NFU
> Michaelmas to Lent
> ride to hounds
> shoot a bit
> and re-arrange a rent . . .

Experts

Talking of ambition (or even delusions of adequacy), brings us to a relatively new performer on the agricultural stage, the *expert*. The all-talking, expense accounted, index-linked agricultural expert, with a BSc, small white hands, and an answer for any question you're likely to ask him. These characters have emerged as farming has prospered. It is awash with cereal experts, chemical experts, livestock experts, financial experts, all of whom would claim some credit for farming's advance into the technological age.

That's fair enough as long as we're aware of three fundamental dangers. One, it's *your* money they're planning to spend; two, their schemes might look good on paper at University, but pretty desperate in a clarty field; and three, even if it *is* a good scheme, maybe not everybody can carry it out.

Let me tell you a little story about the dangers of expert advice, – it concerns a fella called Walter.

Now Walter was the only son of an over-generous wholesale butcher (you will learn quite early in your career that over-generous wholesale butchers are a very rare breed), who set up young Walter in a nice little farm as soon as he'd completed the course at Wallsend Institute of Agriculture. He emerged with a fourth-class diploma, a lot of expensive ideas, and a firm belief that he was about to make a million, while all the other (simple) peasants stood and watched in open-mouthed amazement.

Well, no sooner had he got started than one of those economist blokes, or was he a nutritionist? – anyway he was an expert, mentioned something about an imminent beef shortage. So off Walter went and bought hundreds of little pot-bellied calves and began to stuff them full of barley.

He did the job properly mind, in a couple of months they looked smashing, grand skins on them, full o'fettle. The trouble was the price of beef went down through the floor, and barley went sky high.

Walter put a brave face on it, – 'Not to worry,' says he, 'it's all part of life's rich pageant. . . .'

Anyway luckily he met this big fat dealer from Yorkshire, who as a 'special favour' agreed to take the calves off his hands provided he got a fiver a head luck money, free haulage to Doncaster, and a bottle of gin for his old mother.

The thing to do now, Walter reckoned, was to become one of those immensely prosperous intensive arable farmers. Plough everything, grow wheat 'n' barley. 'Well look at the price of corn now,' he says, 'and I see everybody seems to be gettin' about four tons t'the acre these days, – man it's like takin' sweeties from the bairns. What's more y'only have to work two months in the year, – it's nearly as good as being a schoolteacher!'

However, the seed corn cost a wee bit more than he'd figured, the fertiliser wasn't exactly cheap, and the combine he bought cost the same as a four-bedroomed detached house in the posh end of Newcastle. The barley got mildew, the wheat got yellow rust, the spray price went up the week before he took delivery and, surprise surprise, he didn't get four tons t' the acre after all.

But the bold Walter was undismayed. 'Who cares,' he says, 'look at the price of the stuff, it's on fire and still risin', – by January it'll be like gold. . . .'

Well it might've been if some little bespectacled civil servant with a degree in arithmetic and a fancy woman in Brighton hadn't got his sums all wrong when forecasting the Common Market harvest, and quite forgot about all the grain in France.

Meanwhile those sneaky Russians (for once) got their five-year plan right, and the Americans unloaded most of their surplus at Liverpool. All this news was made public at dinnertime on a Tuesday, and before young Walter had finished his milk pudding the price of grain had plummeted

90

and nobody was at all keen to shift his.

Fortunately though Walter came across a very nice man from the Doncaster area, who having recently bought a big load of calves at a rock-bottom price, was now quite keen to purchase a lot of barley for them at a similarly low figure. Walter, with some encouragement from his bank manager, – did a quick deal.

You had to take your hat off to him, – he took a lot of sickening. After a quick re-think, he came to the conclusion that the only way to make *real* money was to get back into livestock again, but on a super-efficient basis this time. You just had to have more cows and yowes than anybody else; that was the secret, – more livestock units to the acre.

It would all take a bit of organising of course, he would have to sow new leys, get a slick silage set-up, modify the old buildings, buy good livestock, and talk about gross margins instead of old-fashioned profit.

Well there was no doubt about it, Walter did everything right, everybody said so, – the man from the Ministry, the bloke from the University, the chap from the fertiliser firm, and all the other reps who swarmed around him like midgies, – they all said what a tremendous job he was doing.

At one stage he had eighteen cows and calves to the acre, – well . . . only for about twenty minutes actually, – before they ate the hedge and wandered off down the motorway blaring for something to eat.

He managed to raise his sheep numbers to a staggering (and I use the word advisedly), to a staggering twenty-four ewes and twins per acre. Most of them were stone dead of course, but nevertheless people came from miles around to see them eating chickweed and sucking the fence.

However by this time Walter *was* getting a little down-hearted, – after all he'd tried very hard to be a 'super farmer', he'd taken all the top advice. But when he ran out of hay in early February, and that big fat dealer from Yorkshire sent him a load at three quid a bale, he eventually went to pieces and thoroughly clobbered a Jehovah's Witness who came to the door selling instant salvation.

Townie Power

Of all those given to wandering (often uninvited) over your 'Kingdom', probably the most dedicated and irritating is the 'townie pilgrim'. Convinced that the heathen money-worshipping peasant is hell-bent on destroying the country-side, he fights the good fight from hedgerow to hedgerow.

Call him a conservationist or an environmentalist or friend of the earth, or whatever emotive title you fancy, – there's an army of them on the march.

Turn on the telly any night and Attenborough, Bellamy or some other over-enthusiastic creature is photographing the mating habits of a beetle, a baboon, or the lesser web-footed wart-hog. Beats me how the poor things ever mate at all with hordes of nosy TV crews peeping at their every move.

You can imagine some randy old orang-outang chatting up a dolly orang-outang. He's grunted all his sweet nothings, given her a box of Black Magic, turned the stereo and the lights down low, – and suddenly she backs off and says, 'for god's sake Alfie, not now, – Attenborough's watching us from behind that bush!'

Bellamy's more into creepy-crawly things, you see him week after week plodging about in stagnant ponds (in his sandshoes), upsetting the tadpoles.

Then there's the birdwatchers, they're something special, – the keen ones have a uniform, and even the dumbest bird can surely spot them a mile off. They wear massive boots, trousers tucked into hairy socks, a sort of military combat jacket with pockets everywhere, and a bobble hat.

That's not all. They carry a ton of sophisticated watching gear around their aching necks, – special cameras with special lenses, binoculars, reference books, and portable 'hides'.

With all this paraphernalia, they can only move at the pace of a lame hedgehog, – but move they do, all over the place. You may have seen a battalion of them on the News one evening recently, – thousands of 'em had flocked to see some pathetic little bird (who very wisely seldom visits Britain apparently), sitting minding its own business in a hedge in Herefordshire.

'Fantastic,' they all cried; 'how tremendously exciting,' they said. 'It's only once in a lifetime we get to see the spotted tit' (or whatever it was).

The cameras zoomed in to what looked like a thoroughly bewildered and undernourished spuggie, perched on a twig a mile away. The cameras also showed that all these big-booted, hairy-socked fanatics, in their mad intoxicated dash to catch but a fleeting glimpse of this rare bird (who was obviously lost), – had steamrolled through several acres of some poor peasant's barley.

I doubt if they came back to film the crows and pigeons happily feeding on it a week later.

Of course all peasants are not as apathetic or cynical as this. For instance, I know a farmer who is fascinated by owls, – yes owls! To be fair he is quite interested in other species of birds, but the dozy blinking owl is his favourite.

His house is full of owls, – owls carved from wood, owls modelled in clay, drawings and prints of owls. It's only a matter of time before he acquires a talking owl in a cage. As Bellamy is besotted by bugs, this fella is obsessed with owls. The highlight of his life so far is not the day he met his charming wife, or the birth of his delicious daughter, or even the time he got three and a half tons of Huntsman to the acre, – it is the day (he claims), he saw a *snowy* owl.

Now most of us might imagine in our sheltered ignorance that an owl is an owl is an owl. But no such luck, – there are apparently several variations on the owl theme, and the snowy one is very rare. The fact that it's never been seen by anyone else south of Helsinki, only breeds when the temperature's forty below, and there's a total eclipse of the moon, cannot dissuade this man that the pregnant pigeon he saw one night walking slowly up the A1 was in fact this rare and elusive snowy owl.

But they get like that, these wild-life fanatics, – they take on the rampant excited air of people who've discovered something totally new, and treat uninformed bored morons like me as if we were uninformed bored morons.

At least we umpteenth-generation peasants know for sure that life would be much easier with fewer crows, aphids, rabbits, slugs, blue bottles, the local Water Authority, leather jackets, starlings, warble flies, – and maybe conservationists as well. One thing's certain *they* aren't an endangered species by any means, – they must be breeding like maggots. Maybe somebody should film their mating habits.

Perhaps even more numerous are the '*ramblers*', the week-end walkers, and a tremendously influential brigade they are, – their signposts are everywhere. You must have seen them, all those footpath signposts, – they appear quite suddenly. You might imagine that some half-crazed retarded rambler had been creeping about the countryside, planting extremely virile signpost seeds that sprout overnight into seven-foot-high 'trees' with one branch, on which the legend 'public footpath' is already inscribed. Yesterday nothing but a gap in the hedge; today a fancy sign, – the phantom planter strikes again!

What does he look like? Has anybody seen him? Does he wear a mask, a black hat and a cloak, and carry a shining draining spade? Did the Department of the Environment send him? Or is he some lone 'weirdo' with an uncontrollable fetish for sticking poles in fences? How does he get about? On a horse, – a pensioned palomino leased from the Hunt perhaps? Or is he so damned enthusiastic about people plodging about the countryside that he actually jogs from site to site, sneakily eases up a sod here and there, pops in a seed, tramps it in, looks furtively about, and then slopes off into the mist again?

It would be quite exciting if that's the way it was done, – if only because we could then form a peasants' posse, track him down, and shoot him. Alas the truth is much more mundane. Somewhere in County Hall sits a 'footpaths officer', whose job it is to plot and maintain paths, bridges and stepping stones, most of them charted (I suspect), when the only way to get from one place to another was to walk. But the path that once went through the wood, across the burn and over the moor, might now go through the wood, across the burn and over three fields of corn. With all these signposts appearing, the car load who used to just park in a gateway to eat their gateaux and crisps, are now 'invited' to meander much further, – protected by 'divine right'.

That might sound a bit extreme, but there does seem to be a growing opinion that the countryside is everybody's back yard. Well maybe, but it's also the peasant's factory floor, his home, and he's got to make a living there.

A few weeks ago a neighbour of mine counted seventy-five assorted wanderers trekking in quite orderly fashion, as it happens, through the farm buildings.

'Who the hell are you lot?' he asked (a reasonable question in the circumstances), 'and where do you think you're going? There's no public footpath here.'

'Ah well,' said their spokesman, not in the least embarrassed, 'you see we *were* on a footpath, but it seems to have petered out, and as it's getting dark we thought we'd take a short cut back to the road and get a lift.' They went merrily on their way, though just who was going to give seventy-five of them 'a lift' is difficult to imagine.

The signposts that bewildered this small army were apparently erected by another small army, drafted from the job creation or youth opportunity scheme. I spoke to a bloke who saw them at work. Up they drove bright 'n' early one morning (about 11 o'clock), in a brand new van. Half a dozen young men tumbled out the back, produced a tape measure, a hammer, a spade and a signpost, – all eager to plant this totem pole to 'townie power'.

However they were chaperoned by a much older and more experienced foreman, who told them to 'steady down, Rome wasn't built in a day, no need t'panic lads, and how about a cup of tea for starters. . . .'

They never really recovered from this frantic beginning, and took two and a half days to put the signpost into the ground and a couple of rails along the side of a footbridge.

My correspondent assures me it would be unwise to pause on this bridge for a quiet smoke, as the rails are not at all secure; and the signpost, he reckons, will fall in the first stiff breeze, – at which point, he says, he'll chop it up for kinlin'.

Anyway, – be they conservationists, bird-watchers, ramblers or just picnickers, – y'gotta put up with them. After all if *you* lived in the shadow of the gas-works, *you'd* want to go for a walk in the country as well!

The Hunt

Mister fox he would a-huntin' go
into the starry night
to steal a chicken unaware
a triplet lamb alone and spare
a rabbit from a poacher's snare
and home by early light . . .
mister fox he would a-dancin' go
to the tune of the huntsman's horn
a plaintive wind-blown country sound
a scarlet reel for horse and hound
to end in death or gone to ground
all on a frosty morn . . .

You're either *for* the Hunt or you're *agin* it, – very few can stand back and view it dispassionately for very long. Either you consider it an established and colourful part of rural life or, as a peasant, you see it as a diabolical liberty that this amateur cavalry should re-enact the charge of the Light Brigade on your wheat. It may well be magnifique, mais ce n'est pas l'agriculture mon ami!

Three days a week from September to March they emerge (many of them farmers of course), to meet and chase dogs who chase foxes, all under the watchful (blood-shot), eye of the 'master'. Let me 'paint' the scene. . . .

It's bleak early morning, – ordinary mortals are going to work . . . peasants are feeding the livestock . . . children are creeping unwillingly to school.

Major the Honourable Nigel Nicholas, MFH ('Knickers' to his friends), rides proudly out of the kennel yard at the head of the pack. He carries food and drink (whisky laced

97

with cherry brandy), in the large inside pocket of his immaculate red coat, and smokes a long lean cigar. The countryside is only just visible through the chilling mist.

Charlie, the 'Whipper-in', is less elated than the gaffer, so is his mate Alfie the groom. Both have had a 'skinful' last night, and every movement of their mount seems likely to bring on an unseemly disaster.

Charlie is an ex-jockey who had over three hundred rides. His moment of glory (or as near as he got), came when he won a Novices Hurdle at Sedgefield. Now after fifty years astride a horse his knees are almost two feet apart even when his feet are together, and (as had been suggested more than once in the pub), his legs are almost certainly hollow as well.

Alfie spends his days nervously bustling about the stable yard, tugging at his forelock and trying to please 'Knickers', or any other member of the 'gentry' that come his way. This morning he feels 'fragile', but still manages to keep an eye on the master, ready as ever to smile and touch his cap if needed.

Daphne Fanshawe has slept late, and feels like death when finally summoned to 'breckers' at ten. Last night's Hunt Ball has really been 'too much', or at least what she can remember of it, and what she can't remember, doesn't bear thinking about.

Daddy has 'gorn orf' to the city, while mummy (as ever), is hard at work on her daughter, – 'hurry my dear, Steptoe is saddled and ready to go ... jodhpurs pressed, boots polished, and some lovely pheasant sandwiches.'

Down on the farm everything stirs. This is the morning when the staff go about their work in a frenzy, all geared towards putting the boss onto his horse, and out of the yard before eleven.

At 'five to' the boss himself (all seventeen stone of him), waddles out of the kitchen, bearing little resemblance to his weekday working image. He wears the regulation uniform of peaked cap, black hacking jacket (fastened only by the top button), breeches and boots now so tight they might have to be destroyed to be removed.

The tractorman, the steward and the shepherd heave him aboard; the 'odd-laddie' hands up the reins, and the unlucky horse, almost totally submerged, staggers off to the meet, – the boss bouncing along out of rhythm, arms flapping, knees out, 'farming' his neighbour's land as he goes.

This is the day when Roger abandons his act as a hard-working student of agriculture, throws off his oily jeans, leaves behind his battered Ford van and his fractured accent. Puts on his gay debonair rake outfit, the fearless follower of fox and female, and hires a redundant wreck from the lady at the riding school. It doesn't really matter a 'view halloo' if the creature can't break into a sweat, as long as Roger is seen to be there.

If by some miscalculation he does become involved in the 'chase', it might prove embarrassing for both horse and rider. One ploy (perfected now), is to approach the terrifying hunt jump *last*, – politely waiting until everyone else is over and away, then dismount, climb over the obstacle (and still holding the reins), somehow persuade the unladen animal to clamber over after him. Better still, stay on the road chatting up the girl in the TR7.

Fanny, Duchess of . . . (well nobody has ever really been sure where), lives in an unfurnished, unheated stately home, and retains an old seven-horsepower car, and a slightly older one-horsepower horse. She clings defiantly to a way of life she can no longer afford, since the Duke ran off with the family silver and a chambermaid from Wakefield.

A close look at her wrinkled weather-beaten features helps to explain her husband's flight, – and not entirely unaware of this herself, she invariably wears a veil. Yet she still looks impressive on a horse, awesome even; dressed from head to toe in black, she sits side-saddle like some sinister beast from a horror movie.

Knickers gets them all away to the first cover shortly before midday, after the usual free booze provided by an eager tenant farmer, determined to maintain a willing pro-hunt image in a world of feudal one-downmanship.

Thirty riders with a pack of hounds, noses to the ground, unable to see anything farther than six inches ahead, career over the countryside until late afternoon. Knickers blows periodically on his horn, hounds yap excitedly at anything that smells. Charlie shouts and cracks his whip at any dog threatening to chase a rabbit. Most of the time riders stand cold and bored behind a wood waiting for a 'run'.

When it comes, it's Geronimo and the Arapaho nation in full flight. Chiefs on thoroughbreds, spotty children on hairy ponies, peasants on cobs, aristocrats with red coats and blue noses, cursing the gates that won't open, the maiden seeds, the pregnant sheep, and the ocean of winter corn, – all shouting at each other in that special language only 'horsey' folk can really understand.

The 'groupies' who follow in cars jam the roads, park in the back yards of total strangers, and rush to vantage points in three-quarter length sheepskin coats, smiling bravely through the numbing March wind, silently wishing they'd stayed at home to watch Grandstand, or looking for an opportunity to sneak back to the pub before closing time.

Brer fox, he lies low . . . the wise peasant does the same.

However at this stage I must confess to having been part of the hunting scene for a brief disturbed period in my youth.

For three seasons I too plunged over maiden seeds, left undone those gates which I should have fastened, and generally behaved like a mounted moron.

Of course there is a tendency when up on a horse not to see that which stares you in the knee, and one often fails to recognise the real world sixteen hands below.

It was all a bit too upper crust for me, and to be honest I never quite made the grade. For a start while astride the horse I was seldom in complete control, and horses, thick though they may be, are always aware of this. Mine was big, strong, old and evil, and would gallop under low branches and brake viciously at the edge of raging rivers.

The Hunt

I was never suitably dressed for the traditional 'Meet'. Although unmarried at the time, I was nevertheless poor, and couldn't really afford the proper uniform. A spotty youth in wellies, jeans and a cloth cap held on by baler twine, riding a horse in the style of a Mexican bandit fleeing from an enraged posse didn't go down well with the aristocracy.

Those of you who haven't actually 'thrilled to the chase' on the hunting field may be unaware that there are certain rules of behaviour, – and one in particular was the cause of my eventual downfall.

It is written that he who goes through a gate last, shall shut it, and similarly he who opens a gate shall be allowed through first.

Bearing this in mind, it came to pass one terrible cold and rainy day in January that a very distinguished gentleman of great importance, superb breeding and immense wealth, led a large group of riders to a gate in the corner of a field.

The gateway was a mess, a sea of clarts and muck, where lots of cattle had stood quietly abluting all winter long.

This distinguished gent, having arrived first, carefully leaned over his horse's neck, unhooked the chain, and gingerly reversed, opening the gate as he went. The others stood back patiently to allow him through, according to the rule.

It was at this moment that a figure in a cloth cap tied on with string, riding in the unmistakable style of a Mexican bandit, on a horse completely out of control, appeared from nowhere travelling at great speed. He roared through the mire, and through the gate (so conveniently open), leaving desolation in his wake.

Everyone, particularly the distinguished gentleman, was covered in . . . well, call it 'slurry' if you like.

I might still have got away with it in the blind confusion that followed (for a while everyone had their eyes shut), – but once through the gate, my horse declined to go any further.

Hell hath no fury like a bunch of Rt Honourables covered all over in smelly dark green stuff.

I took up golf shortly afterwards.

Politics

The politician told the farmer
in the spring of '84
the larder is a-burstin'
and we don't want any more –
he said you're far too bloody clever
you've now grown quite enough
the milk is over-flowing
and the gran'ry's full of stuff
we've got mountains high of butter
and a lake of surplus wine
tons of cheese and powdered eggs
all buried down a mine –
just what we're gonna do with it
we haven't got a clue
so for God's sake stop producin'
and just enjoy the view –
yet half the world was starvin'
in the spring of '84
politicians didn't hear them
gently knockin' at the door . . .

No serious comment on the farming scene would be complete without some brief mention of politics. Yes, I'm aware it's a painful subject, – dull, boring, devious, and awash with scoundrels.

Somebody once observed that politicians only reach such elevated positions of importance, because they have no talents to detain them elsewhere.

This is probably true. However you can't ignore them, they're unlikely to go away, – and now with a European

Parliament as well, there are even more of them about, constantly blathering predictable rubbish, generally debating themselves into higher office, and the electorate into a deeper hole.

Nowhere is this more apparent than in agriculture. One year they may encourage you to produce more milk or corn or potatoes, and generously 'bribe' you to do so. The next they'll decide there's far too much grub in the larder and introduce quotas, clawbacks, devalue the green pound, and spend the money on rockets instead.

Any peasant who attempts to keep pace with the seasonal whims of the political machine is likely to end up confused and broke. Common sense and a straight answer are seldom part of the political animal.

Consider for instance the glittering career of Sir Charles Hardly-Able, until recently the Rt Hon Member for Tow Law and Ebchester.

It was always predicted that Hardly-Able would go right to the top, and no one at Westminster was in the least surprised when the PM rewarded him with a knighthood in the latest New Year's Honours List.

After all he'd been at the Department of Irrelevant Affairs for over a decade, and could justifiably claim the major credit for the Department's emergence from a little one-room office in Pontefract, with a part-time secretary called Mabel, to the vast concrete complex it now was, covering three hundred acres on both sides of the Thames.

Even he had realised at an early age that destiny would lead him to the political arena, – his pathetic school reports confirm this.

After failing to acquire any form of gainful employment (except for a brief spell as treasurer of the Local Leek club), Sir Charles sprang onto the first rung of the political ladder, and was elected to the Parish Council. The fact that there was a big 'suckler' sale on election day, and only three people voted, did nothing to mar his joy.

For the next couple of years he tried vainly to persuade the vicar to build an international airport next to the village hall, and negotiated with ICI to move their chemical plant from Billingham to behind the Black Swan. They declined.

However failure never dampens the blinkered enthusiasm of the politician, – obviously a man of such vision couldn't be held back for long, and the ever-alert Party machine soon adopted him as a parliamentary candidate.

That first election campaign was really the beginning. Few people now remember how with hard door-to-door pestering, rare eloquence, immense charm and a pack of lies, he was swept to Westminster.

His maiden speech was sensational. Before a packed Commons, who'd sat all night hurling abuse at each other, he spoke for an hour and a half without anyone having the faintest idea what he was talking about, and received a standing ovation from the front bench. The PM was very impressed, 'Hardly m'boy,' he said (it was a 'he' in those days), 'that was brilliant, – in fact I haven't heard a more meaningless speech since Michael Foot was in his prime. Keep it up, the party needs men like you.'

In the next cabinet reshuffle he became an under secretary at the Ministry of Employment, and together with Arthur Standstill of the TUC, devised a new social contract which guaranteed sickness benefits, non-contributory pensions, free milk and a colour telly to everyone who turned up for work on alternate Tuesdays, if it wasn't too cold.

Success was now inevitable, and a spell at the Foreign Office confirmed his growing appreciation of International affairs. He might well have achieved Ambassadorial levels, but for his careless reference at a Kremlin reception to Mr Brezhnev as 'a four-eyed Commie git'. Later the same evening Sir Hardly was photographed in compromising circumstances with a Russian truck driver . . . called Natasha.

Such indiscretions as these made him a natural choice for the Defence Ministry, and from there he was subsequently elevated to Chancellor of the Exchequer (on the strength of his earlier experience as a Leek club treasurer), – and finally to the prestigious DIA.

Sep met Sir Charles Hardly-Able at the Clartiehole

Conservative Fête. Normally he wouldn't be seen alive at such an event, but Gladys and her mother wanted to go, and Sep had been persuaded to deliver and collect them. He soon lost patience when they failed to appear at the agreed 'pick-up' time, and set off in search, wandering rather nervously into the crowd of well-heeled party faithful.

The Honourable Nigel Nicholas was shepherding Sir Charles across the lawns, introducing him to eager ladies in twin-sets, who all smiled and said how privileged they were to meet the great man, shook his hand coyly, and retreated into little bunches to twitter about how distinguished he looked.

'Ah Sep, how nice to see you,' said 'Knickers', breezily. 'I don't think you've met Sir Charles, have you?'

'How are you?' beamed Sir Charles, looking straight past Sep towards a predatory photographer from the *Clartiehole Gazette* (for a moment Sep thought the man must be cross-eyed).

'I take it you're a committee man' (the politician had long since mastered the art of smiling and speaking at the same time), 'how splendid,' he said, 'jolly good show. . . .'

He was about to move charmingly onwards when, realising that the man hadn't even seen him yet, Sep said, 'I'm certainly not one of your mob bonny lad, – in fact I reckon all you politicians should be hoyed in the dipper. . . .'

'Absolutely,' beamed Sir Charles, who hadn't understood a word, 'keep up the good work, there's a stout fellow. . . .'

'Hi, wait a minute,' shouted Sep, 'that's the trouble wi' you lot, – you're so busy blatherin', y'haven't time t' listen.'

'Couldn't agree more,' smiled Sir Charles, searching above and beyond Sep's cap for his chauffeur, 'time is of the very essence. Indeed as I said at the Blackpool conference in '79, – we must all pull together, backs to the grindstone, elbows to the wall to make a better Britain for the poor and the aged and of course our children and our children's children . . . and . . .'

Sep tried to stop him in full flow. 'If I ran m'farm like you lot run the country, I'd be knackered in a twelvemonth,' he said, quite steamed up.

'Absolutely, jolly good,' smarmed Sir Charles, 'so nice to have met you, . . . er . . . Mr . . . er, . . . and do keep up the good work. . . .' And slowly realising that here was something less than an ardent admirer, he turned to his host, – 'Knickers old man, I fear we really must be orf, important debate in the House tomorrow y'know, – my speech may be decisive, what, ha ha ha.'

Sep watched him go, – grinning his way towards the Rolls and a place in history.

'Jesus,' he muttered quietly, 'I've got a collie dog brighter than that bugger, . . . and with a bit o' luck Sweep won't write his memoirs!'

Seasons

'Pet Lamb'

*He was born alone and friendless
on a wet'n windy night
and his mother died unaided,
apparently from fright —
so we brought him in half perished
and tried to set 'im on
to a mule who'd hanged a single
buried dead and gone
but the bitch was quite determined
that she would not be 'used'
and she kicked the little bugger
'til he failed to be amused —
so we fed him on the bottle
as he piddled on the mat,
which soon upset the labrador
and prop'ly huffed the cat —
but he lived somewhat reluctant
sucking everything in sight,
ate herbaceous borders
and bleated half the night —
we kicked him and we cursed him
always scratchin' at the door,
the postie ran him over twice,
he still came back for more —
pot-bellied and peculiar
he just refused to grow,
a hungry little nuisance
till the time he had to go —
by the winter he looked better
eating turnips, nuts and hay,
but he crept into the grain store
and blew up on Christmas Day!*

Spring, the poet tells us, is the time when young men's thoughts lightly turn to a bit of what they fancy. Well that may be the case with poets and academics, who wander about lonely in a cloud meditating on daffodils, red red roses, and the picture on page three of the *Sun*, – but be assured once you embark on a career in peasantry, spring is more likely to strangle your libido, and addle your imagination. You have something else on your mind, – it's called panic. It's the same every year: a snowdrop comes up in the garden, a couple of spuggies chat each other up in a dry gutter above the back door, four midgies are seen dancing down by the grain shed, and a civil servant puts the clocks forward, – this is it.

Rumours begin to filter through that someone has been seen cultivating land, or spreading white granulated gold on his winter barley. The March wind is mopping up the clarts, the ploughed land turns from black to grey to white, and the bloke up the road has twenty acres of oats sown already.

Filled with fear that you may be left trailing in the Peasant's Spring Handicap Chase, – you begin to rush about like a blue-arsed fly, oiling this, greasing that, fixing things, discovering breakages you should've mended before Christmas, and others specially created by the gods to slow you down. Tractor batteries suddenly go flat, tyres go hiss in the night, there's a world shortage of bearings for your discs, the telephone's out of order.

Desperately you get things more or less organised and move onto the starting line with the others, engines revving.

One final check, though. You have a proper look at the land after supper, you kick it, turn it over; yes it should 'work down' alright, – well maybe *hardly* dry enough really, hasn't been much frost this winter, – but you can't wait forever, even the cultivator's getting itchy feet. Right then, that's it, you'll start tomorrow, – could well have forty acres sown by the weekend and all the winter stuff top-dressed.

Next day the snowdrop has withered, the spuggies are

sheltering under a hemmel roof and the midgies are dead, –
'cos it's snowing!

Two weeks later you start again (pointing out that those
who *did* get some spring work done a fortnight ago were far
too early, and serves them right if all their nitrogen is
washed away down the drains).

You rattle about in a safety cab listening to the weather
forecast and Dave Lee Travis for two days and two nights,
until you produce a tilth capable of growing prize leeks.

At midnight you can hear the rain pelting on the bedroom window, and your prize tilth is semolina.

Spring is a mischief.

Meanwhile the yowes, unaware of your other problems
(and not very interested either), might begin to lamb, or on
the other hand they might not. The beginning of a lambing
is seldom short of trauma.

I remember meeting three neighbouring peasants one
day in March. The first man should've started a fortnight
earlier, but nowt had happened. 'Oh they're in lamb right
enough,' he said, 'but that fancy tup w'bought last September must've missed them all first time around!'

The second bloke was in a hurry. 'Can't stop,' he said,
'they're droppin' like flies, – four pairs and a three this
mornin' already, and two more messin' about, – gotta
go . . .!'

'Sounds like a canny start,' says I.

'Y' think so,' he said without enthusiasm, – 'they're not
due for three weeks yet,' and then as if anticipating the next
question he added, 'randy hogg wi' one stone from next
door!'

The third fella had a familiar problem. He was feeding
some hoggs on the last of the turnips one bright crisp
morning when lo and behold, there were two little new-
comers who'd arrived during the night.

Nobody claimed them of course. Their mother (busy
stuffing her face at the troughs), certainly wasn't interested,
denied all knowledge of the happy event, apparently viewed
them as intruders from outer space, – and when eventually

caught (after wrapping herself up in the electric fence), she proved to be as lean as wood, and as 'milky' as a brick.

The man was pretty philosophical about it really. He did the only reasonable thing possible in the circumstances, he lost his temper and tried to kick the hogg to death. All he achieved of course was a sore foot (he was only wearing wellies). The two additions to his flock were both half-perished, and the size of undernourished gerbils. It took several days of intensive care and half a bottle of gin before they were persuaded to live.

Personally I think the most desperate lambing I can recall was as a raw eager youth working for my father.

He must've had some kind of brainstorm, or maybe it was just a clever ploy to get rid of his wayward son, – but that year he decided to treble his yow population, and divide an endless lambing into three parts.

First (in early Feb), came the Cheviot hoggs.

Now I don't know if any reader has ever had much to do with Cheviot hoggs (chances are he'll be in a rest home now anyway), – but let me tell you that breed of sheep (more than most) is especially designed to induce premature heart problems. You've gotta get up very early to get the better of those creatures. They travel at the speed of light, propelled by a constantly revolving tail, – with a demented gleam in their eye, a total lack of maternal instinct, and a conviction that the shepherd is out to slaughter them all.

By the time I'd finished lambin' two hundred of them, they weren't far wrong. I was a decade older and speaking to nobody.

But that was just the beginning. No sooner had they been 'dealt' with, than the main flock of half-breds came in. They were enormous walking white billiard tables, who lived only to eat.

They were a lot slower, easier to catch (harder to cowp), but still with that inbred talent to drop dead for no apparent reason, – they would limp about with their 'back-body' sticking out like the brake lights on a motor bike, and produce triplets while firing on one tit. It was quite a normal lambin' with them I suppose.

Then came the Blackies.

I don't know where he'd bought them, but their one overriding ambition was to get back there.

You never knew where they were, – fences were a minor irritant to them, a feeble challenge to crawl under or leap over. Perhaps it was the lack of bracken or heather and open spaces that confused them, but whatever it was, they certainly weren't settled and happy 'in bye'.

They lambed anywhere except the lambing field, – in somebody else's lambing field maybe, under a thorn bush, half-way up a tree, all over the place. Bring them into the stackyard at night, and like Apache Indians who fear the confines of a reservation, they'd creep off silently before dawn, taking any new lambs with them, heading west again into the badlands.

But by the end of April it was more or less finished, – the seeds full of twins, singles on old grass, the gelds cashed, the dead buried, the straw pens burnt, – and half a dozen pot-bellied pets eating the vegetables in the garden. That's spring.

> *Sun is shinin'*
> *clover cracklin'*
> *rowed up clean and bright*
> *the forecast says*
> *it should stay fine*
> *at least until tonight*
> *baler greased*
> *and off we go*
> *(leave the headland last)*
> *by dinner time*
> *there's twenty bales*
> *and eighteen shear bolts smashed*
> *just twice around*
> *by two o'clock*
> *broken bales and string*
> *nuts and chains*

and spanners lost
kick the bloody thing
now cloudy sky
a cooler breeze
feel the rising panic
run back home
phone out of breath
and plead for quick mechanic
hang about
while neighbour's hay
is baled up like a train
mechanic's here
at half past five
and with 'im comes the rain. . . .

Spring inevitably gives way to what we euphemistically call *summer*, and some of the pressure is eased (warm disasters are better than cold ones), – and peasants begin to talk to their wives again.

If spring be the season when things agricultural come to life, then in summer you must concern yourself with keeping most of them alive, – so that you can cash something come autumn. Just because everything's looking green 'n' lovely one day in May, doesn't necessarily mean you're in for a good year.

On the other hand, one dead yow doesn't make a summer either.

Perhaps the best writer on rural subjects was A. G. Street, and one of the pieces he wrote years ago dealt with this fatalistic view of the farming year.

Every year is different he reckoned (no argument there), and there's nowt much you can do about it. The seasons come earlier or later, or all together. The lambing is good or moderate or 'canny', – the politicians are generous or mean or blind. Mother Nature smiles benevolently, or plays hard to get.

However there's one thing you must try to do, he said, and that was to get things as 'right' as you could by June, – that's the watershed of any year.

You can understand what he meant, – by June you'll have sown the spring crops, top-dressed all the corn and grass, probably sprayed against disease and weeds, hopefully done the jobs as well as you can, – and that effort will largely determine the harvest.

Alright, the weather can still knacker the crop before you harvest it, but you've no chance of a decent crop at all, if you haven't done the basics, – by June.

I suppose he would have argued that cattle well bought, ewes well kept, silage sweetly made, a good crop of lambs onto their feet by late May, early June, – lays some sort of foundation for the year as a whole. What you need after that is a bit of luck.

But no matter how promising the picture looks, ignore all predictions from whatever source.

It's almost inevitable that you will come across an article in February, written by the agricultural correspondent of some national newspaper, forecasting a bumper harvest for British farmers this year. Now if this scribe worked for a comic paper you might be a trifle sceptical, but chances are he's with some highly respected Daily, so you may well be fooled into thinking he knows what he's talking about. He doesn't, – how could he? We probably haven't sown half of it yet, and in any case still to come are March winds, April showers, mildew in May, thunderstorms in June and July and a broken combine in August.

Not that it worries him of course, – if he's proved right, he'll pen a modest little piece in September beginning, 'as I forecast way back in February . . . etc, etc,' – and if he's wrong he produces an even smaller piece beginning: 'Owing to the drought, the floating Deutschmark and a wildcat strike of welders in Warrington, the harvest has failed to fulfil its early promise . . . etc, etc.'

It's much harder though to ignore the peasant from over the hill. Whether you're a beginner or a veteran, he'll be watching you – and you'll be watching him, though you might not admit it.

For instance, there I was one pleasant July afternoon

with a knapsack sprayer on my back, quietly plodging through the vast sea of nettles that each summer threaten to take over the old stackyard, looking a bit like a lost astronaut, when the car drove up to the gate.

He came over (this fella from up the road), stood on the windward side of the drift, and nodded.

It was a couple of minutes before he said, 'have y' sprayed anything else lately?'

'No,' I said, '. . . well except for a few boar thistles in that field over there, that's all, . . . why?'

'Y' haven't sprayed any wheat?'

'No.'

He lit a cigarette, taking his time about it.

'Is it alright?' he asked ominously. 'The wheat I mean, alright is it?'

'Looks alright to me,' I said. 'You can see it from here, quite a nice crop I think. . . .'

I tried to sound as confident as I could, even tried to inject a touch of apathy, – but I recognised the first twinges of peasant panic nibbling at my stomach.

'Aye, *ours* looks pretty good from the road,' he said.

'What do y'mean?' I was getting worried. The knapsack was beginning to splutter, and so was I.

'Well,' he said with infuriating calmness, 'you'll have heard of Septoria, I suppose.'

'Oh yes,' I said, 'I've heard of it.'

He drew slowly on his cigarette . . . 'know what it looks like do y'?'

'Well it's like, er, y'know . . . it's er, well it's a sort of, er, – fungicy thing, isn't it?'

Hardly a scientific answer, but I was looking anxiously towards the nearest wheat field now, expecting it to turn a dirty brown colour before my very eyes. No, it still looked fairly green . . . though maybe hardly as green as it did twenty minutes ago.

'Well there's a lot of it about,' he said, 'thought I'd better warn y'.'

'Thanks,' I said, swallowing hard, 'I'll have a check

114

through it t'night.'

As soon as his car was out of sight I was frantically groping in the bottom of the crop. I saw imaginary diseases in there I'd only heard of and certainly couldn't spell. Was that rust, or eyespot or Rhynchosporium, – or this dreaded Septoria? Anything that wasn't the purest green began to look like some devastating malady, – could it all be a 'write-off' by the weekend?

At dinner time I phoned our friendly neighbourhood spray expert.

'Septoria?' he said. 'Yes there is a bit of that about this year, – I'll come and have a look tomorrow night if you like.'

'Tomorrow night's no bloody good,' I screamed, 'it could all be rotten by then. Come now!'

Nevertheless he came the next night and wandered about knowledgeably looking at the leaves, while I followed like a little schoolboy waiting for a bad report.

'Well,' he said eventually, 'there is a little bit, but nothing serious, – I wouldn't spray it yet.'

'Are y' sure?' I asked, some relief spreading back to my stomach.

'Yes, it's OK,' he said. 'You don't want to spray just for the hell of it do you? – But by all means get another opinion if y' like.'

It seemed a good idea, and next morning I took an armful of wheat to a man at the Ministry laboratory. He looked at it carefully through a microscope and said, 'It's *all* got Septoria, – spray the lot or you are doomed!'

I went home feeling like a condemned man, and found another Ministry man (from another department), waiting to see me. He was there to take more samples as part of a national wheat disease monitoring scheme (I'd been picked out of the ADAS hat purely by chance).

'You couldn't have come to a better place,' I said miserably, 'seems my wheat has every disease in the book.'

'Looks alright t'me,' he said, 'a wee touch of Septoria maybe, – but nowt t'worry about.'

'*Nowt t' worry about!*' – he must be joking. Who the hell do you believe? To spray or not to spray, – either decision could be right (or wrong), it's one of the many occasions when you get the feeling you're hardly clever enough to *be* a peasant.

As it happens the wheat *was* sprayed, it seemed it might be the lesser of two evils, – but perhaps we've all been 'programmed' now to inject everything that moves, and spray anything that doesn't.

However the point of this little tale is just to illustrate the kind of pressure faced in summertime . . . 'when the livin' is easy' . . . and everybody else is on a topless Spanish beach.

Autumn, that season of mellow fruitfulness, sounds as if it should be a time for 'easing off'.

The harvest safely gathered in, the livestock looking full and fit, still in summer coats, the kids back to school (at last), – the days getting shorter, and the tempers a little longer.

Well it maybe used to be like that, way back when simple peasants simply sowed all their crops in spring, and harvest was an end to the farming year. When corn was sold, lambs cashed, fat cattle marketed, the tup 'put away', – and the bank manager pacified for another twelve months.

Not any more though.

Now autumn is the season of frantic activity. No sooner is a crop cut than the fires are lit and in goes the plough again. There's a mad dash to sow the oilseed rape, more winter barley and wheat. Time is short, it could start raining tomorrow and forget to stop . . . what's the forecast?

So the machinery howls far into the night, the telephone almost melts. Where's that seed, – you promised it last week! Where's that mechanic, – the tractor's stood idle for half an hour already! Where's that corn cheque, – I need it to buy more fertiliser!

It's a time when time is always threatening to run out, – and it does of course, when *winter* comes a-sneakin' in.

Winter should be abolished, along with nuclear weapons and formation dancing, and I include here a poem by Thomas Hood who, presumably sore depressed at the prospect of waiting forever for spring to come back again, wrote the following as the year began to die.

> *No sun, no moon,*
> *no morn, no noon,*
> *no dawn, no dusk,*
> *no proper time of day, –*
> *no shade, no shine*
> *no butterflies, no bees*
> *no fruits, no flowers*
> *no leaves, no birds, – November?*

I know how he felt.

One old peasant acquaintance who achieved little fame as a poet, reckoned, 'we generally get seven months of winter, – and five months of bad weather. . . .'

Winter is that long journey through short days, – hungry days when cattle blare to be fed (like young children), and greedy sheep knock you over at the trough. You feed them all in the bleary half-light of dawn and dusk and New Year's Day.

It's when water and diesel and old knees freeze, when it's difficult to start a tractor (or yourself). Everything is harder to do.

And as if that wasn't enough, – right in the middle of it all we get Santa Claus!

Gardening

When the new peasant moves into his new farm, he will discover an enclosed area adjacent to the farmhouse which could well give him more trouble than all the rest of his estate put together. It is called the garden.

It's just possible of course that the last bloke was a little green-fingered fanatic, and there's a ready-made 'lovesome thing, god wot', – on the other hand the 'thing' could be entirely out of control, clawing at the front door, and tapping at the living room window.

Fortunately, having myself recently moved across the yard to another house, I can readily appreciate the problems associated with a virgin garden.

Now there are romantics (would you believe), who imagine that fairies live at the bottom of all gardens. Well perhaps (I can't pretend to be too familiar with the life-style of fairies), but as far as I'm aware the only thing at the bottom of ours is a septic tank, which at best would suggest that if all gardens *do* have fairies at the bottom – our fairies are probably smellier than most.

As this is written, the septic tank is undeniably the outstanding feature of the garden, – it's a great big ugly slab of concrete with a manhole cover at one end. It sticks up like the tomb of some long-gone Egyptian potentate (perhaps we've got pharoahs instead of fairies . . .).

Anyway this is a very young garden, raw and inexperienced, like a callow youth, and I (like most peasants), am a rather unenthusiastic gardener, who might, on good days, be inclined to wander through it conjuring up visions seen in Sunday colour supplements (a rose or a flowering shrub over there, a lupin or a petunia here perhaps), – but without any real knowledge of the subject.

Gardening

Are all farmers poor gardeners I wonder? – No that can't be right, I've seen some impressive farmhouse gardens, but then perhaps the wife did that.

My father claimed you couldn't be a good farmer *and* a good gardener, – the two jobs just didn't go together. He'd reinforce this argument whenever some unfortunate bloke was late with his harvest, or didn't get his turnips sown on time, or got 'caught' with a field of hay. 'Well, what y'expect,' he'd say (all superior), – 'spends all his time in the garden, doesn't he?'

Mind you, if anybody was visiting us for supper, somebody was quickly detailed to cut the lawn, trim the privet, weed the gravel path, hack down the nettles round the apple trees, and generally tart the place up. 'I always like to see a tidy garden,' he'd say, – as if he'd done it all himself.

All peasants are like that to some extent, – it just seems more sensible that the other 300 acres (or whatever), should take priority. After all there is an outside chance of that area making a bob or two, – the garden's only gonna give y' back-ache.

The trouble with *our* garden then (the one with the smelly fairies), is that it's about thirty years since it *was* a garden. Once upon a time it did actually grow assorted veg, but since then mother nature has been responsible for it, – and she obviously believes in letting everything go to seed.

So where do we start? Well disregarding the old joke about a load of green ready-mixed concrete, laid with a tap in the middle to wash it down occasionally, and possibly a plastic pansy tied to the tap with red baler twine to add a little colour, – the first job was to get rid of all the dockens, dandelions and 'auld man's baccie'. So out with the knapsack again, and spray everything with Roundup and diesel. After that I set fire to it, and it was exciting for a minute or two, – in the blaze a fork lost its shank, a plastic clothes line melted, and I think I heard the fairies coughing.

Having removed all the surface debris, you then have to dig it over, and the spade shank snaps, the prongs on the new fork bend, boulders creep to the surface, along with bits of pram, bicycle, ancient farm machinery, chains, wire, old horse shoes (these you must spit on, and hoy over your left shoulder for luck) and bones, – we unearthed millions of bones. One might have been persuaded this had been an ancient burial site, but before I'm overrun by eager archaeologists, let me assure you they are not the remains of neolithic man, or a lonely centurion, or even a missing master of foxhounds, but simply the bones of a few knackered old mule yowes, and a very good collie dog I buried there m'self, after he was run over by one of those old Fordson tractors with iron wheels.

So now we've got it all tidied up, what next? A lawn perhaps? Yes a lawn would be nice to relax on (three days a year), a good idea, – but resist the temptation to buy a five-year ley more suitable for three cuts of silage and strip grazing cows in the autumn. Get some proper lawn seed, even though the price per square yard will leave you breathless.

Then off to the local garden centre for some bonnie little bedding plants with strange sounding names. Here I have to admit my knowledge of plants is limited, – I can recognise snowdrops and fat hen, but that's about it, consequently any nurseryman who can twitter on about Saxafridgia and Amaryllis (and spell them properly), is onto a 'good thing' with the likes of me.

Anyway I do know you need some tall wobbly things at the back, little fluffy stuff at the front, creepy crawly bits for the wall, a bush or two scattered about, and an old sheep trough at the door perhaps (with droopy things falling over the sides), – and slug pellets everywhere.

In its third year, our garden is definitely taking shape. Who knows in a couple of years it could be open to the public at 50p a time, – I bet they're getting worried at Blenheim and Kew already.

Meanwhile I'll have to cut the damn lawn again (maybe half a dozen sheep would do the job), and I still haven't worked out how to disguise that septic tank. How about a posse of gnomes standing on top of it, – holding their noses of course.

After Hours

As soon as you become a fully fledged peasant, you may well be persuaded to join a number of organisations connected with farming, and if you are what's known as a 'committee man' you'll have plenty of chances to go out every night. If on the other hand the incessant chatter of grown-ups behaving like juvenile politicians bores the knickers off you, then best settle for dominoes and drink instead.

Scene 1. The local village hall on a wet Monday night in October, where in a steamy smoke-filled room next to the Ladies toilets, the Clartiehole and District branch of the NFU are holding their monthly executive meeting. Everyone, all seven of them, who regularly attend this gathering, are all talking at once about the price of mutton, and how Charlie Thompson (who isn't present of course), still has a field of barley to combine.

'Best of order *please*,' says the chairman, 'it's time we got a start, – are there any apologies . . .?'

'What for?' asks a voice from the back row.

'Absence, y'silly bugger,' says the chairman. '. . . No? right then, we'll take the minutes of the last meetin' as read, and if you're all agreed, I'll sign them. . . .'

'When are the union gonna do somethin' for us hill farmers?' shouts a red-faced fella still wearing his cap and an enormous top-coat.

'Never mind about you lot,' says a milk producer, – 'you're subsidised every time you blow your nose!'

'It's us beef blokes what's gettin' clobbered,' says an eloquent gentleman at the front, 'us is lossin' money hand over foot!'

'Order please,' says the chairman. 'Can we have the delegate's report, Ernie?'

Ernie has been to the county executive meeting where he slept soundly most of the time, but luckily for him the county secretary sends him a copy of the minutes which he now reads. One of the essential qualifications of an executive delegate is an ability to read.

'We discussed warble fly eradication,' he drones, 'and a resolution was sent to London we also discussed wild oats and sheep scab and milk quotas and intervention prices and four other resolutions were sent to London there was a report on conservation in Gateshead and we discussed that programme on television about rich farmers then we . . .' He says it all without a comma.

'Thank you, Ernie,' says the chairman, 'are there any questions?'

'Aye,' says cloth cap with top-coat, 'when are they gonna do somethin' for us hill-men?'

'T'hell wi' you lot,' says the 'gentleman' at the front. 'It's us beef blokes what's gettin' clobbered. . . .'

'Is there any other business?' asks the chairman wearily. 'If not I declare this meeting closed.' But nobody's listening, they're all blatherin' on about the price of mutton, and how Charlie Thompson's still got a field of barley to combine.

Scene 2. The clean and newly swept concrete farmyard of Jeremy Kneeless-Browne, top farmer and President of the Clartiehole and District Meadow Fescue Society, where tonight he will conduct a farm walk and 'talk-in' around his splendid establishment.

You're in classy company here, – all the energetic, cost-conscious, gross-margined, forward-thinking farmers are gathered together, discussing their fourth silage cut, and how many ewes and twins can be stocked, paddock grazed on tetraploid. (At this early stage you decide to keep quiet, having made mouldy hay, and seen your own sheep wandering about thankful for a nibble of Yorkshire fog and redshank.) The others however go on talking about their unique herd of Simmental cross Charolais Chianina bull calves, giving a liveweight gain of two stone a week, and the incredible price per kilo they received at the sales last month.

They'll modestly announce how their winter wheat yields are always about double your own, thanks (they'd tell you) to new varieties, timely fertiliser application, selective spraying and perfect management.

Young Kneeless-Browne confidently answers all the complex and sometimes awkward questions. Even when it comes to queries about his rent (a secret generally guarded with one's life) or his bank loan, or his profits, – he glibly pours out the required information. Not once does he tell anybody to mind their own bloody business, – he's an open book. How much is fact and how much fiction you have to decide for yourself, – but you're likely to be impressed, you may even be jealous.

Don't be. The history of farming is littered with 'geniuses' who had more machines than sense, and more buildings than brains, and ended up with a lot less money than you. Remember that the traditional worried, run of the mill peasant maybe seldom hits the jackpot, – but he doesn't often 'go down the Swanee' either. No, don't join that club, it's too dangerous especially for a beginner, – you might get ideas above your overdraft.

Go on, join the Leek club instead, or take up karate (it could be useful at clipping time), – or go to night classes in embroidery, you can get *too much* agriculture y' know. Well pitmen don't go visiting coal mines on their days off, do they? (sometimes they don't visit them on their days on either), – you don't often see a plumber inspecting other people's U-bends on holiday. When a train driver knocks off does he go home to play with his model railway? – I doubt it.

Other people, ordinary folk (not farmers I mean), only work when they're absolutely forced to, – the rest of the time they go to the pictures, or play Bingo, or have a fortnight on the Costa Brava.

Some even take their wives out for a drink at weekends, but perhaps that's taking things a bit too far, – no need to go completely berserk!

Holiday

Farmers are 'conditioned' to view holidays on a par with smoking marijuana and nude bathing. Even in this more enlightened sophisticated age, the myth persists that any form of leisure activity unconnected with agriculture indicates laziness, incompetence, or just more money than sense.

The truth is that a lot of farmers simply don't *want* a holiday; a few days away from their 'kingdom' is a sentence, and while they're serving it, the farm will undoubtedly go to rack and ruin in a matter of hours. The wickens will multiply, the harvest will rot, the yowes will abort, the staff will do nowt, the house will be burgled, and the postman will run over the collie dog.

Any farmer who *is* persuaded (or blackmailed), to fly off to Greece or Grimsby, or wherever, generally keeps it secret as long as possible, and is consumed by guilt for months afterwards. His mates tend to view him with a suspicion usually reserved for drag artists.

'Good god, you've been on holiday have y'?' the sordid truth leaks out, and is greeted with the ridicule it deserves . . . 'How the hell did y' manage that?' And then just to make the villain feel truly degenerate . . . 'I've never had a day off in fifty years!'

'Why not?' you ask naïvely.

'Why not?' He laughs as if faced with an idiot and a cheat. 'Because we can't afford it, that's why not, – haven't got the time either . . . better things to do than lie about on the beach y'know.'

You might reasonably think that any job that allows no free time and no spare cash can't have much going for it, –

but that's not the real reason that keeps the peasant at home. It's this misplaced arrogance that he's indispensable, coupled with hereditary meanness. After all everybody else is actually *paid* to have a holiday.

We're all tarred (more or less), with the same brush, – and if as an 'undergraduate' peasant you haven't been affected yet, – you will be. . . .

Sep was one of those farmers who'd never had a holiday, – never really wanted one, not a proper one anyway, not in a posh hotel, *for a whole week!*

Fair enough going down to Smithfield with the 'lads', that was alright, – a wander round the fancy machinery, a look at those pampered cattle, a few pints and an embarrassed stroll around Soho. But away (with the wife), for seven days, – that was too much, what on earth would they talk about?

'We can't afford it,' he said at the start. 'Have y' any idea what it'll cost? – a fortune, a bloody fortune! Yes, I know everybody else has a holiday, but they're different.'

'We'll go in June,' said Gladys, 'before the harvest.'

'Impossible.'

'It'll do y' good,' she said, 'y' need a break.'

'Rubbish.'

'I fancy Scarborough m'self,' she went on undismayed, 'or maybe Scotland . . . but no, Scarborough would do nicely. . . .'

'What about the clippin'?'

'I'll phone up t'night and book somewhere.'

'. . . and there's that hemmel t' muck out. . . .'

'I've got the brochure here, – there's some lovely hotels in it.'

'Who's gonna shut the hens in at night? The fox'll get the lot y' know. . . .'

'How about the Imperial? – that looks nice. . . .'

'What about the kids though?' he asked, desperately.

'Mother says she'll have them, – they like goin' there. . . .'

'What if there's a foot 'n' mouth outbreak while we're away?' He was panicking a bit now.

'It'll be smashin',' she twittered.

'Or fowl pest.'

'I'm really lookin' forward to it.'

'Or aphids.'

'It'll be like a second honeymoon.'

'Jesus,' he said, 'that does it, – we're not goin'!'

The morning they set off was marred by Sep's predictable churlish behaviour. At breakfast he claimed he had an ulcer, toothache, lumbago, and possibly a fractured left thigh. Later he came in declaring that all the cattle were developing signs of pneumonia, and virtually the entire sheep flock had destroyed a fence and were grazing the wheat.

Gladys ignored him.

Overnight it seemed the turnips had been attacked by a plague of flea-beetle, and an army of leather-jackets had emerged from the bowels of the earth, intent on consuming all the barley.

She finished packing, humming 'Fly me to the moon,' and for the only time in living memory, was ready to leave first.

They made several abortive attempts to drive out of the yard, – he'd forgotten to lock the desk, he'd forgotten to feed Sweep, to switch off the electricity, dose a calf, stop the papers, and leave the hotel phone number with Willie in case he was needed in a hurry.

It took three hours to get to Scarborough, during which time Sep said not a word, and the car never exceeded thirty miles an hour.

On arrival his disposition hardly improved. He told the wine waiter what to do with his bottle of Nuits St. George, and 'downed' three pints of Newcastle Brown over dinner, then three more as he watched Match of the Day in the TV Lounge. He complained every meal time that the menu was in 'fancy French' while the food was 'ordinary English'.

'Continental breakfast, sir?' enquired the waiter on the first morning, – he wore that condescending smile waiters often have when serving peasants obviously out of their depth.

'What sort o'breakfast's that?' snapped Sep, who'd been up since six o'clock looking for some grass to walk on.

'Coffee and roll, sir,' smiled the waiter; 'the usual.'

'Coffee 'n' bloody roll,' exclaimed Sep, 'y'mean a cup o'coffee and a bread bun for breakfast? No wonder the Common Market's in a mess if that's all they have in the mornin'!' He looked sternly at the waiter. 'I want a bowl o' porridge, a plateful of bacon (crispy), a tomato, two eggs, some fried bread and a pot of tea (hot)!'

He turned to the old dear on the next table who was trying hard to ignore the outburst while reading the *Guardian*, – 'Porridge is the stuff, isn't it, pet,' he said confidentially, 'puts a linin' on your stomach.'

The only other person he spoke to was a businessman, who claimed he also had an interest in a dairy farm in Hampshire and an uncle who was a farmer in Dorset. But as soon as Sep discovered the man was inclined to stand up when women-folk came to the table and called his wife 'darling' all the time, whatever they might have had in common soon evaporated.

Gladys managed to persuade him down to the beach one very hot day, and what's more he took his cap off almost immediately, – revealing the dramatic frontier between weather-beaten unhappy face, and the pure white of his brow above and beyond.

Later he took his jacket off, and shyly slipped his braces from his shoulders, looking furtively around as he did so, like a seductive stripper removing the seventh veil. Then he fell asleep. In fact, he slept a lot, both indoors and out, often creating some confusion with his weird open-mouthed mutterings. One afternoon, while snoozing in the cloistered silence of the residents' lounge, he suddenly stiffened, and in a voice that would be heard in Filey, screamed, 'git away bye, Sweep!'

He payed the bill at 7 am on the last morning. 'Do you realise,' he said to the unfortunate receptionist, 'do you realise I could've bought a right good bullock for what I've spent here, – a right good 'n!'

They were on the road home by 8.30, and Sep sang all the way to the back door.

The Thibenzole rep was waiting nervously in the yard, preparing himself for the usual salvo of abuse, no sale, and a quick getaway.

'Morning,' smiled Sep, 'fancy a cup o'tea bonny lad?'

The Heavy Fantastic

It's a well-known fact among peasants, that as soon as you take off your comfy, filthy, smelly working clothes, have a quick wash (a bath even, especially if the lambing's just ended), – and put on some fancy 'goin' out' gear, – not only will you feel most uncomfortable, but you'll damn near freeze t' death as well. This is a fundamental reason why the peasant remains scruffy and reluctant to venture farther than the nearest mart. Further unnecessary acts of gallantry, such as taking the wife out, are not only a threat to his chauvinist life-style, – they could become habit-forming and a danger to his health.

The night of the Clartiehole and District Rabbit Clearance Society's Annual Dinner Dance was cold and miserable, and as he got ready, Sep felt very like the weather.

The suit, bought in 1947 for cousin Elsie's wedding, and worn since only for funerals, was laid out on the bed like a thin black corpse, – the clean white shirt hung ghost-like from a British Rail coat hanger on the wardrobe door. He had three ties, – one shiny silvery number for nuptials, a shiny black one for burials, and a shiny stained YFC tie for all seasons.

When he came downstairs Gladys was standing smiling hopefully in front of the cooker, waiting to be told how splendid she looked. The brand new creation bought specially last week under the strictest secrecy revealed about three acres more of her than she normally dared, – but after all Sep had said it was about time she 'sharpened herself up a bit,' – he'd be chuffed with this outfit.

'Socks,' he said, like a surgeon demanding a scalpel, 'I haven't any socks.'

129

Gladys's smile faded, as she produced a drawerful for him to choose from.

'Right then,' he muttered, 'are y' ready?'

'Been ready for ages,' she said, thoroughly huffed, and went out to the car.

The car however was in the hayshed, and she was half-way across the yard, marooned like a whale on a mud-bank, before she realised she was in a sea of clarts, – but she swam on bravely (silently).

They entered the dining room of the Black Swan, both with stony expressions and dirty feet, – her's hidden to some extent by the long dress, Sep's fairly obvious, because he'd rolled his trousers up a good six inches to display not only muddy shoes, but one green sock and one maroon.

He bought a port and lemon for Gladys and a pint for himself, and stood back to the bar surveying the scene.

'I don't know anybody here,' he said, '. . . Oh thank God, there's Willie, we'll get a chat with him, – he doesn't like dancin' either, – and there's Charlie, I'll maybe sell 'im some hoggs before the night's out.' Perhaps it wouldn't be too bad. He got another beer.

'There's little Jackie whatsisname, always shoutin' and swearin' and bossy at the mart. Look at 'im now, – he's holdin' that chair for his missus to sit on, mind she's a big 'n isn't she . . . maybe he'll pull the chair away just as she's gonna settle . . . no . . . I thought he wouldn't.'

Sep lit a cigarette, 'I see Tommy's here . . . is that his wife done up like a Ming vase? Must cost a bloody fortune to keep her . . . serves 'im right though, standin' there orderin' whiskies for all his huntin' mates . . . bet they gallop over his seeds in the mornin'. . . .'

He got another pint and suddenly realised he was ravenous. It was past his bedtime, never mind his supper time. There was one of those buffet affairs laid out at the far end of the room, and already a crowd was helping themselves. Sep joined them and managed to collect about a 'buck-rake' full of assorted pies, sandwiches and cold meats onto his plate.

He was eating his third trifle when the band 'struck up', and Gladys asked him to dance.

'Got a bad leg, pet,' he said apologetically, 'I'll get y' another drink though. . . . Willie, get some drinks in bonny lad, we'll have a kitty. . . .'

The Terence Sickley Three were known far and wide for their all-round musical ability to play anything from 'heavy-metal' to the St Bernard's Waltz. (The fact that whatever tune they were playing sounded remarkably like the one before, – and the one after, – didn't seem to bother their fans.)

Terence himself thumped his way up and down an ageing upright piano. A very large female accordionist, who because of her immense bosom, would have been well advised to consider a less dangerous instrument, sat in melancholy mood beside him.

And to complete the ensemble there was Ernie, a manic drummer, who beat out the same 'haunting' rhythm regardless of the dance.

'Take your partners for the eightsome reel,' shouted some sadist, who obviously had no intention of performing anything so foolish himself.

He left them to it, – screaming women were hurled carelessly about by red-faced men with jackets off and sleeves rolled up especially for the job in hand. Every set gave a different interpretation of the steps.

When it ended the bar was overrun for fully half an hour. Half an hour after that, the Gents was overrun as well.

At two o'clock in the morning Sep suddenly decided he wanted to dance after all. By this time of course Gladys didn't, – but he insisted noisily, and together (more or less), they demonstrated a highly sophisticated Latin-American manoeuvre, while the rest of the crowd stood watching, rigidly at attention, as soon as they realised the Terence Sickley Three were in fact playing 'God save the Queen'.

On the way out Sep slipped his arm around Gladys. 'Well, pet,' he said, '. . . it wasn't half as bad as I thought it would be . . . did y'enjoy yerself . . . and is that a new frock y've got on . . . ?'

131

Eating

Of course dancing was never a very likely after-hours pursuit for peasants, – they seldom have the feet for it. Eating however *is* considered an acceptable activity, and peasants are quite good at this, always have been. In fact anyone who doesn't clean up all his greens and milk puddings can never be taken seriously as a peasant.

Habits may have changed a little over the years, but generally speaking the traditional farmhouse eating routine is regular and constant.

My father (and most of his generation), would get up about six o'clock and immediately have a mug of tea (his mug was about the size of a forty-gallon drum), and perhaps a piece of his favourite fruit cake. Out he'd go to feed the sheep or whatever, – and come back in promptly on eight for a second 'proper' fried breakfast (with mushrooms if he'd found any), and more tea.

Mid morning (about 10.30), he'd be back for another mug-full and perhaps another piece of his favourite fruit cake. This would keep him going to dinner time, at noon, which would consist of cold beef or mince or sausages, followed invariably by rice and prunes. He would be out again at one o'clock on the dot.

Tea time came round at 3.30, a brief but essential break, taken inside or out depending on the work in hand.

Supper was at 7.30 pm and was more or less a repetition of the mid-day meal.

Predictably after all this work and food, he would fall asleep in his chair until woken up just before bed-time with another 40-gallon mug of tea. How he slept all night with that load aboard I'll never understand, but he did.

You will gather from this that the good lady of the farmhouse was fully employed either preparing food, serving food, or tidying up after the consumption of food. If on top of that she had a couple of kids coming home starving from school, two or three pet lambs to feed, the calves and the hens to look after, – a quiet night out at a restaurant, being waited on, must have been a very special event.

For the modern peasant, dining out may hardly be such a unique treat, but for the more traditional variety it's still a rare occurrence, – generally requiring (on the part of the wife), plotting, blackmail, subtlety, and careful planning on a par with the preparations for the D-day landings. . . .

It was a Friday, and Sep had sold a few sheep at the mart. The lambs made a fair enough trade, – but the highlight had been the achievement (it was nothing less), of persuading two geriatric mule yowes actually to walk into the ring unaided. What's more they managed to stay upright until they were sold, and minutes later the pair staggered out again (coughing in perfect harmony), and Sep found himself twenty quid richer than he had any right to expect.

Perhaps it was the euphoria of this minor miracle, but he made his first mistake when he got home, – he told Gladys about it. She said nowt, but she had the twenty pounds 'spent' before the kettle boiled.

Later they were watching an old film on the telly, when she eventually broached the subject. On the screen a real smooth bloke with bags under his eyes was whispering romantic rubbish to a glamorous creature (falling out of her dress), while they nibbled away at a candle-lit champagne supper in a luxurious apartment overlooking the Seine. They'd obviously had a splendid nosh, and a few bottles of 'bubbly', – but old smoothy still looked hungry, and was staring lecherously at the lady's obvious charms. The massed strings of the Watford Philharmonic played softly in the background. It seemed the perfect opportunity for Gladys to attack.

'You never take *me* out t'dinner,' she said.

Sep appeared to go into a sudden deep coma.

'I said we never go for a meal anywhere do we? Willie and Florence are out every Saturday night . . . but we never go out . . . never!'

Sep made his second mistake, – he came out of his coma. 'That's a lie,' he said, 'a downright lie. You're always exaggeratin', – what about the time I took you to see Sound of Music?'

'That was in 1969, – and anyway it doesn't count, 'cos you went to sleep. I'm talking about eating out.'

'What about last week?' he demanded coolly.

She was ('almost'), speechless. 'We bought two cold pies from the Take-away comin' back from mother's, and ate them without stopping in case you missed Sportsnight!'

'Well what about that day at Hexham?' he snarled.

'Y' can't count that either,' she said, 'a ham sandwich and a Penguin biscuit in the mart canteen is hardly dining out,' – she was warming up now. 'You know what your trouble is, don't you? – you're just mean!'

She went on for quite a while, and by the time she'd finished the couple on the telly had walked off up the Champs Elysées, and Sep had reluctantly booked a table for two at the Queens Head.

On the big night Gladys was all smiles. She smiled at the 'flunky' who took her coat, she smiled at the head waiter who called her 'madam', she smiled at the couple on the next table, she even smiled at Sep. 'Isn't it lovely here,' she smiled, 'and haven't the waiters got such lovely manners? . . . they're all French you know.'

'They're all bloody queers,' muttered Sep.

One of them left the menu and waltzed off to the kitchens, another offered the wine list and hovered, pencil poised.

Sep looked at him in the manner that generally removed persistent salesmen, but this fellow didn't go away. 'Would monsieur like something to drink?' he asked.

'Pint,' grunted Sep.

'Monsieur?'

'And half a shandy for the missus.'

'We'll have nothing of the kind,' smiled Gladys effortlessly, and ordered a bottle of Saint Emilion '76 and two Croft Originals for while they were waiting.

The waltzing waiter returned for the order.

'I'm not hungry,' said Sep miserably.

'Of course you are,' insisted Gladys. 'C'mon what do y' fancy?'

'Mince 'n' chips!'

'Monsieur?'

Gladys was only a little less calm. 'You can't have that,' she smiled (more weakly now), 'let me see the menu. Yes, I'll have the Pâté and your Poulet Suprème,' she announced in the voice she reserved for the vicar, 'and my 'usband will have the vegetable soup and a nice fillet steak,' and looking menacingly across the table she added, 'well done!'

The sherry was long gone, when the wine, suitably warmed, was brought in. 'About time,' said Sep, 'I'm parched.'

The wine waiter poured a thimbleful into Sep's glass and waited for the verdict.

Sep waited too, and looked up expectantly at the bottle.

'Would monsieur like to taste the wine?'

'Of course I'd like to taste the stuff,' he growled, 'but there's not enough there for a spuggie. Leave the damn bottle and I'll help m'self!'

Gladys, undismayed, and still smiling bravely, leaned over the table as provocatively as she could, remembering the glamorous lady on the telly, and whispered, 'what shall we talk about then?'

'I'll have to take m' jacket off,' said Sep.

'Don't you think it's nice to come out to a place like this . . . just the two of us . . .?'

He took his tie off as well.

'I mean the staff are so helpful, and clean, and smart, and nice, aren't they?'

'Wogs,' he said.

'So what'll we talk about?' she smiled with determination.

Sep, however, was now demolishing his steak, and he'd

acquired a taste for the wine. He'd ordered another bottle together with some more 'taties' (a request which seemed to confuse the staff for a moment or two). He polished off a vast meringue glacé cum knicker-bocker glory concoction after that, and attacked the cheese board and a brandy while Gladys blathered on about how nice it all was.

'Now didn't you enjoy that?' she said when he finally leaned back and loosened the top two buttons of his fly. . . . 'My chicken was delicious, and the peach melba was . . . Sep, – Sep . . . you're not asleep are you?'

He stirred, grinned a disorientated grin, and looking straight past her into the middle distance he raised one arm and bellowed, 'Garcon, le pint s'il vous plait, et une demi shandy pour ma femme!'

Gladys, overcome with joy, leant forward and kissed him on the nose.

The Young Farmers

They drive too fast it canna last
they're out most every night
they're all the same life's just a game
and father's never right
half a chance they're at a dance
you don't know where they've been
swingin' free 'til half past three
stone deaf and in a dream
they're judgin' cows or clippin' yowes
support the local club
drinkin' mates heavy dates
a dart match at the pub
courtin' strong knew all along
another wedding soon
but not today we're baling hay
wait 'til after June
committee meetings public speakings
trip to USA
a twenty-first a headache nursed
through the working day
barbecues and Christmas do's
does money grow on trees
is this a race can't stand the pace
burnt out at twenty-three . . .

Most farming families encourage their offspring to join the local YFC, believing that it's marginally better for young Willie to be *there* than at another teenage orgy with evil glue-sniffing townies. Young Willie of course does everything he can to sustain this belief, because he's quite happy

137

with the weekly 'goings-on' at his local club, under the guise of a debate, a quiz, or whatever.

Father of course was a member of the organisation years ago (there was little else to do then), when the programme was entirely devoted to calf-rearing, judging Ayrshire heifers or cross Suffolk gimmers, and a series of long-winded lectures on the love life of the liver fluke . . . or so he'd have you believe, – but older men tend to have convenient memories.

Anyway the movement has had to change that image. Nobody in their right mind is going to leave their fireside and the telly, to venture forth on a bleak winter's night, and listen to some fanatic waffling on about 'worm infestation', in an unheated sixteenth-century church hall.

However they haven't forgotten their rural background, and the modern young farmer still indulges in the more traditional pursuits such as stock-judging, snoggin' in the back of an Escort, and public speaking.

The first real speech I ever made was in a YFC competition. You know how it is when you first join *any* organisation (NFU, WI, Rotary or whatever), – you sit quietly in the back row trying to be unobtrusive, terrified that if you so much as cough or break wind, you'll immediately be put on the committee. String two coherent sentences together and you're chairman for life.

Presumably I must have created some kind of disturbance, – and having been 'noticed', was promptly entered in the club team. The rules stated that this team consist of three: a chairman to introduce the proceedings, keep a semblance of order, and sum up at the end; a speaker, who in those less liberated days generally gave a fascinating five-minute talk on 'fowl pest', or (if he was a real rebel) perhaps something avant-garde like 'a day at the mart'; and thirdly someone to perform the most difficult task of all, – the vote of thanks. Precedent indicated that no matter how abysmal the speech might be, the appreciation should be euphoric. Even if the audience were fast asleep, had gone to the pub, or were rioting in the aisles, the vote of thanks to the poor gibbering nervous wretch who had just spoken had to leave no one in any doubt that here was a youth destined to be Archbishop of Canterbury (or at worst a superintendent with the Water Authority). Sometimes it wasn't easy to sound convincing.

Anyway on this occasion I got the job of 'speaker' (can't remember what the subject was), a canny quiet lad called Matthew was detailed to give the vote of thanks, – and the chairman chosen was an 'alleged' female called Anne.

I say 'alleged' because at that stage nobody was very sure about her gender (or indeed all that interested). You see Anne was one of those aforementioned 'horsey' girls. She lived and breathed gee-gees, and would turn up at our practice meetings, direct from the stables, dressed in wellies, filthy old anorak, shapeless jeans, and smelling of horse liniment and saddle soap.

We practised in a back room of the Nags Head twice a week. The sessions lasted about ten minutes, before (in despair) we would adjourn to the bar. We knew we were bad, and getting worse, and eventually a couple of nights before the competition, we panicked and sought professional advice. He was the English teacher from the grammar school, keen on speech and drama, and was only too pleased to be involved.

I remember he listened to our efforts in bewildered silence.

'Well?' we asked him, 'are we as bad as we think we are . . .?'

'Yes,' he said.

'Is there anything you can do for us at this late stage?'

'No,' he said . . . 'at least nothing as far as the performance is concerned . . . in fact the only thing I can suggest is that you smarten yourselves up considerably . . . you all look destitute, like refugees, – especially you,' he said, pointing at Anne. 'You can't go up on stage looking like that, what on earth will the judge think?'

Matthew and I took the warning seriously, we didn't want to make any bigger fools of ourselves, – the 'speechifying' was bad enough. So we duly dressed ourselves up on the night, and just hoped that Anne would make some kind of effort as well.

She was late, our team had just been called, when the doors of the village hall opened and in glided this film star. For a moment we didn't recognise her without the anorak and jeans, she looked like several million dollars. Whoever was responsible for the hair-do and the make-up job knew their business. Her dress was a long black number, sprayed on, with a neckline that plunged to the navel, and a split in the skirt that tried desperately to reach that area too. I particularly remember three strategically placed sequins, and an innocent smile.

To cut a long story short, our team performance was farcical, but the judge couldn't take his eyes off our chairman. I don't suppose he heard a word of the speech, Anne just fluttered everything she had, and we won by a mile.

My first YFC competition of *any* sort was a sheep clipping contest, and it wasn't so successful. I'd been taught to clip (or shear), at home of course, where we had those enormous half-bred ewes, and my instructor was an enormous half-bred shepherd employed by my father at the time. Norman, that was the man's name, had a very simple technique. He would storm into the catching pen (no sneaky looks for an easy bare-bellied sheep), grab the first animal to hand, render it virtually unconscious with a swift upper-cut, and have the fleece off and wrapped up before she came out of the coma, – 'nea bother at all'.

But *he* was far bigger and stronger than me, indeed so were the half-bred ewes, – and they always presented a major challenge to a raw youth.

Consider my relief and delight then, to discover that the sheep to be clipped at this competition were 'Blackies'. I knew nothing about their temperament or their fleece but obviously they were only half the weight and size of the monsters at home, and what's more, they had 'handles'. I fancied m' chances, it looked easy.

So with the rest of the club looking on, together with a

few parents and a judge, half a dozen of us grabbed a sheep each and prepared to impress the gallery.

'Are you all ready?' said the judge, – 'go!'

I'd no sooner got mine 'opened up' around the neck, than I realised to my dismay she had one of her horns fast in my flies, and as I paused momentarily to consider the implications of this, she went away. She just got up and went away, – taking with her a substantial and important section of my trousers.

Farming's like that, – it's never easy to hide your inadequacies.

Dig

Some deep rural thinker once advised his audience to 'live as if you were gonna die tomorrow, and farm as if you would live forever'.

The first half of this philosophy could be dangerous of course, especially if (on the basis that you wouldn't be around to face the music), you were persuaded to assassinate the landlord's agent, run off for a dirty weekend with the milkman's wife, give all your barley to the poor in Ethiopia, and shoot your neighbour's randy tup.

The second half may make more sense, – but as you speed through your roaring forties (and discover it's becoming more and more difficult to catch a lame yow without the help of a good dog and a young posse), as you clutch your bad back and second hernia, there comes the realisation that 'for ever' isn't quite as long as you once thought it was. Other peasants will farm this plot after you, – several generations have done so already.

This fairly obvious fact was brought home to me a few years back, when a group from the University undertook an archaeological 'dig' in the front field.

They knew something was there before they started of course, – aerial photographs showed a pattern of dark rings on the brow of a small hill. Before you could mutter 'nil illigitimus carborundum', a man from a ministry had decided there was a Roman Fort buried beneath.

The Professor and his gang of students arrived in the spring, arranged for a few inches of topsoil to be removed by a twentieth-century JCB and proceeded to search systematically for centurions.

The two-acre site was undoubtedly the poorest, stoniest

bit of land on the farm, and it was a slow job. A yard at a time on dimpled knees, trowel in hand, they scratched away looking for recognisable evidence that someone had lived here long long ago.

Recognisable to *them* that is. At first it was just an old piece of pottery, which in fact looked nothing like an old piece of pottery, unless you particularly wanted it to. Then an occasional bit of crude glass would appear, which I suggested might be from an old Tizer bottle, but they insisted was certainly Roman jewellery.

They dug up bones too. What faith they had. 'Goat perhaps, or deer,' they said, 'or even some great hairy creature long since extinct . . . second century BC.'

'Mule yow, early Brewis,' I suggested, but they weren't listening.

However, piece by piece, square yard by square yard, a pattern that even I could recognise *did* emerge, and the professor was now quite sure that this was an early *British* settlement. He was quite excited about this, because apparently almost every ancient site of this kind is immediately labelled as a Roman Fort (whether anyone actually digs it up or not), – and as he pointed out, ancient 'Brits' were here long before Caesar.

This then it was decided was a native set-up, where indecent law-abiding early Geordies lived and worked, and drank the occasional pint of 'mead'.

Here they were minding their own business when along came the Romans, who probably pinched a few sheep, chatted up the local maidens, and moved on for a punch-up with those kilted heathens over the wall.

The settlement remained until the people were driven out by another tribe, or smitten by a plague, or simply emigrated to a more sophisticated site further south.

Anyway you could picture the scene easily enough once the soil had been removed, there was a definite pattern of stones and old timbers. Perhaps six or seven circular huts, twelve feet across, – in the centre, evidence of a fire. Outside, the dwelling area was surrounded by a ditch, and a few yards further out, another one, – two lines of defence against marauders.

The 'Prof' reckoned the livestock were brought into the compound between the two ditches at night.

Almost as interesting as the 'dig', were those who dug, – especially the girls. During a glorious spell of weather through late June and early July they crawled about in bikinis, getting browner every day.

We were making hay in the next field at the time, and no hay ever received more care and attention. It was wuffled to death, and everybody was disappointed when we finished leading it in.

However by the next spring the site was back to normal, covered up again, and the ghosts sleeping quietly under the barley.

It's a sobering thought though, that two thousand years ago another bunch of peasants were scraping a living just a couple of hundrd yards down the road. I wonder if a thousand years from now some Professor and his bikini-ed students will dig *this* farm up. They'll be wastin' their time. They won't find any coins or jewellery from my era that's for sure, and most of our pottery is cracked already. Any glass they find will almost certainly be the remains of non-returnable empties, and the bones will be lambin' casualties.

They might be confused when they uncover the ruins of our old backyard 'netty'. 'Obviously some sort of shrine,' they'll say knowledgeably, 'perhaps a place of deep religious significance . . . probably where the simple old peasant went to contemplate in times of stress. . . .'

They wouldn't be far wrong.

All That Glitters . . .

I recall when I was small
and safe on mother's arm
how long I dreamed for years it seemed
to farm a little farm
'was just a fool who stayed at school
when all the world was turning
hay to bale and lambs for sale
thorns piled high for burning
tales to tell and smells to smell
sweet dew on the morning clover
red skies at night the rare delight
of days that just rolled over
business now – profit now
the honey is seldom so sweet
the grass ain't as green as it was in the dream
– but who wants to live in a street . . .

To sum up all this 'enlightened' rubbish then, – just what is it that makes one farmer different from another, what sorts out the successful and the indifferent, the sheep from the goats, the men from the boys . . .?

It's not as simple as one might imagine.

It's not necessarily the number of cattle he keeps, or the shine on his machinery, or even the thickness of his crops, and just because he drives a supersonic Italian car and lives like someone from the cast of 'Dallas', doesn't prove much either.

There's not two alike really, – some are owners, others tenants; some started off with a bank full of money, others with less than nowt. But when we talk about the basic 'character' of farmers there are (arguably), only two camps.

There's the progressive bunch (who don't *always* progress mind you, but look and sound as if they do), and there's the peasant. He probably doesn't appear to be very 'with it', – but often survives just as well and maybe longer.

Nothing's certain though. A progressive can sometimes progress too far and fall over the edge of his imagination; a few peasants get stuck in the clarts and sink slowly out of sight.

Anyway, this progressive character (or as the press call him, 'top farmer'), is easily distinguishable. He may well do a great deal of hard work, but he hates to give the impression that he does anything other than manipulate his empire from beind a computer and a forest of filing cabinets. His every-day appearance is designed to accentuate the contrast 'twixt businessman and mere farmer. And business-man is what he is.

As a result commercial travellers call him mister, or even sir, – and only mention his christian name when telling lesser mortals how they've just sold him a hundred tons of fertiliser or a bag of dog biscuits.

He does most of his buying and selling through groups, syndicates and big anonymous co-operatives, and has a built-in fear of marts. This is primarily because it's there he meets the unscrupulous devious peasant farmer, – though he'll pretend it's because he believes the whole mart system is out-dated and inefficient. What's more, he'll tell you, he hasn't time to stand about gossiping all day, because he's meeting this chap from ICI to talk over nitrogen require-ments, or a man from the University is dropping by to chat over his costings.

The peasant, on the other hand, hates getting dressed up in any way, convinced that if he remains scruffy, everyone will come to the conclusion he works like a mad thing nine days a week. He'll wander around with a hammer in his hand, looking for something to 'mend'. His pockets are full of bent nails, nuts looking for single unattached bolts, bolts looking for unmarried nuts, a length of baler twine, and a bone-handled pocket knife (with the bone half gone, and the blade snapped).

He is attracted to marts like a moth to a light.

It's the place to compare those half-truths, to swap exaggerations and collectively 'pray' for the early downfall of the local whizz-kid who seems to be doing far too well.

'Progressive' talks a different language. He'll worry right through June about the dry matter content and digestibility of his silage (and how many cuts he'll get), – whereas ordinary peasants tend to be satisfied with good hay or bad hay (once), and refer to it as 'canny hay', regardless.

'Progressive' is constantly concerned about the daily liveweight gain of his intensively reared calves, – others see at a glance that they're 'doin', or they're 'not doin'.

'Progressive's' enormous flock of brand-new super-ewes Mark 2, especially bred by some redundant chicken sexer down south to withstand anything that nature can throw at them, and still live on virtually nothing while producing a 300 per cent lambing crop, – are fed the optimum scientifically balanced ration and kept indoors three deep. This is considered absolutely essential in order to make them what his economist friend calls 'a viable proposition'.

The fact that half the ewes die (for no reason the economist can think of), and the other half have no milk and end up with a 100 per cent crop, only helps to convince the management that the solution to the problem is twice as many super ewes Mark 3.

The peasant, as most of us know, simply gets on with the job in the time-honoured thoroughly inefficient way, and has either 'the best lambin' ever', or 'very *nearly* the best lambin' ever', – whatever the end result.

It doesn't really matter a hoot which camp *you* think you belong to, – and any assessment of a successful farmer by others is pure guesswork anyway. Mercedes and Martinis can often mean just a .big nasty overdraft, and a beat-up Ford Popular and the occasional pint can mean exactly the same.

I once asked a wise old peasant what *his* definition of a good farmer was. 'Well now', he said, 'I think if y' can make a few quid, and leave the place a bit better than y' found it, – y' haven't done s'badly. . . .'

That sounds about right.

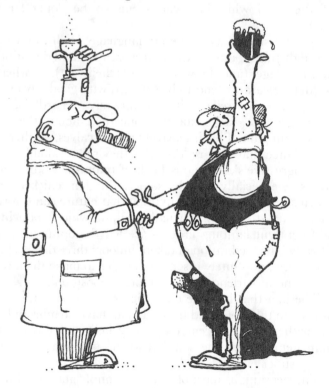

Glossary . . .

of some obscure North country and/or farming words to be found in this book, which may confuse the suburban reader south of Darlington.

ABUSED: Treated badly, – which in the context of sheep usually means starved, mismanaged, and a stocking rate as thick as flies. (Conversely, it can also mean treated too well, – so making it difficult for a new owner to sustain the lifestyle.)

BAIT: Refreshment, often taken to place of work in a 'bait-tin', or a 'bait bag'. Sometimes eaten by collie dog when you're not looking, or run over by your mate on the other tractor.

BLACKIE: Blackface sheep, usually found on hill land, – just as diabolical as any other breed.

BLATHER: To talk incessantly about very little, or even nowt, e.g. economists, reps and some women are prone to 'blather'.

CHASER: Usually refers to a castrated male sheep used to tease or excite the female of the species, yet obviously unable to become a dad. However, in some areas a chaser is simply one that has not been castrated *satisfactorily*, and so *can* become a dad (and often does). Furthermore, it is not unknown for this word to be used in a human context as well, but we won't go into that.

CHEVIOT: Yet another breed of sheep, – this one is virtually wild.

CLARTS: North-east mud, – found in gateways, farmyards, and occasionally on living-room carpets.

COME BYE T' ME HERE:
Instruction given to a collie dog, in the hope that it will return to its master, e.g. 'come bye t' me y' donnered animal!'

COWP: Turn over. Sheep are 'cowped' to clip, or to inspect their rotten feet, or to administer some medications. Some sheep 'cowp' independently, – and stay that way.

DONNERED: Singularly unintelligent, thick.

DOON BYE: (Or in-bye), refers to lower-lying land, generally more fertile and the farming more varied. 'Oot bye' (or out-bye), is the higher ground where only the hardier breeds of sheep (and peasant) can survive.

GELD: Strictly speaking it means to castrate, – but it can also refer to a yow that produces nowt at lambing time.

GUFFIE: A pig.

HECK: (Or rack), a container for livestock to eat hay (or wickens) from.

HEMMEL: Cattle yard or court, a building to house cattle during the winter. The older examples are often so small you can't get the muck out, and the more modern ones so big, no one can afford to buy the livestock to fill them.

Glossary . . .

HOOND: A hound, or dog (in some areas the word dog is pronounced durg).

HOY: Throw, or hurl.

LUGS: Ears, usually those of an animal, and often used for the implantation of identification tags, other marks, and hormones; in sheep, sometimes removed by inexperienced shearers.

MULE: Sometimes known as Greyface, another breed of sheep, a killer.

NETTY: A small detached 'convenience' often situated at the bottom of a garden, sometimes referred to as a 'privy'.

NOWT: Nothing, of no significance. Example: 'the promises of a politician are worth nowt.'

PLODGE: A useful descriptive word, meaning to walk or trek (in wellies) through clarts. Each step taken sounds like 'plodge'.

RAKER: A term used to describe a sheep that wanders (or rakes), refusing to be confined in one particular field. Sometimes the word is used in a human context: for 'field' read 'bed'.

TEK THE HUFF:

    (Or take the huff): a term used to describe a malady peculiar to sheep. The symptoms are a refusal to eat or move, and although a thorough veterinary examination may reveal no known disease or infection, the animal will expire when it's good and ready. Sometimes referred to as 'bloody awkwardness'.

WICKENS: Wicks or couch grass, . . . like the 'Hunt', imposs-ible to ignore, and of no practical value.

WUFFLER: A remarkable machine that prepares hay for the baling process, and then encourages rain.

YOW: Ewe, female sheep (to be avoided whenever possible).